One Life at a Time, Please

BOOKS BY EDWARD ABBEY

NOVELS

The Fool's Progress
Good News
The Monkey Wrench Gang
Black Sun
Fire on the Mountain
The Brave Cowboy
Jonathan Troy

ESSAYS

One Life at a Time, Please
Slumgullion Stew: An Abbey Reader
Beyond the Wall
Down the River
Abbey's Road
The Journey Home
Desert Solitare

NATURAL HISTORY & TRAVEL

Desert Images (with David Muench)
The Hidden Canyon (with John Blaustein)
Cactus Country (with Ernst Haas)
Slickrock (with Philip Hyde)
Appalachian Wilderness (with Eliot Porter)

Edward Abbey

One Life at a Time, Please

An Owl Book
Henry Holt and Company   New York

Published by Henry Holt and Company, Inc.,
115 West 18th Street, New York, New York 10011.
Published in Canada by Fitzhenry & Whiteside Limited,
91 Granton Drive, Richmond Hill, Ontario L4B 2N5.

Library of Congress Cataloging-in-Publication Data
Abbey, Edward, 1927–89
One life at a time, please.
1. Abbey, Edward, 1927–89—Biography.   2. Authors,
American—20th century—Biography.   I. Title.
PS3551.B2Z47   1987   813'.54[B]   87-8812
ISBN 0-8050-0602-8
ISBN 0-8050-0603-6 (An Owl book: pbk.)

Henry Holt books are available at special discounts
for bulk purchases for sales promotions, premiums,
fund-raising, or educational use. Special editions
or book excerpts can also be created to specification.
For details contact:
Special Sales Director, Henry Holt and Company, Inc.,
115 West 18th Street, New York, New York 10011.

Most of the essays in this book first appeared, in abridged form,
in various magazines, newspapers, and other publications. For
permission to reprint them here, the author thanks the publish-
ers and editors of the following: *San Francisco Examiner,
Northern Lights, Harper's, The New York Times Magazine,
Mother Earth News, National Geographic, Arizona Daily Star,*
Houghton-Mifflin Co., *Architectural Digest, Earth First!, City
Lights Review, Bloomsbury Review,* the University of Arizona
Press, *New Times,* Northland Press, and the National Broad-
casting Co.

Designed by Kate Nichols
Printed in the United States of America
10   9   8   7   6

This book is for
Clarke my wife,
and for our children—
Susie, Rebecca,
and Benjamin

O Lord, make me an instrument of thy peace.
Where there is hatred, let me sow love;
where there is darkness, light; and where
there is sadness, joy . . .

—*Saint Francis of Assisi*

Contents

Contents

One Life at a Time, Please

Preliminary Remarks

*T*his book consists of a collection of occasional pieces, most written on commission from some magazine editor, book publisher, or college speakers bureau. Whether or not each piece rises to the occasion I leave for the reader to judge. All were written for money, in the higher, finer sense of that ambiguous term—I have a wife, an ex-wife, several children, a dog, a cat, a mortgaged house, and a 1973 Ford pickup truck to support—and all were written for fun. I would like to think that some of these compositions attain the dignity of the essay. If not, they qualify at least as "literary journalism" and are eligible thereby for reproduction in book form. Whatever the case, some background information should be useful to the reader in understanding their peculiar tone and tenor.

My favorite essay in this book, "Immigration and Liberal Taboos," is also the one with the most colorful history. I wrote it on assignment from the editors of *The New York Times* Op-Ed page. Having agreed on topic and length, I scribbled the thing down, typed it up, and mailed it off as requested, that is, "as soon as possible." In my case the job took about six hours. I waited for the response, the cheery letter of acceptance, the handsome check. Days passed. Weeks. Finally, two months after mailing in the essay, I received a letter from one Gideon Gill at the *Times* saying that the editors liked my contribution but would I please reduce it to one-half of the previously agreed-upon length. Annoyed but still eager to see my views printed in the august editorial section of the *Times*, I retyped the piece, deleting (in effect) every other sentence, a few adjectives, and two jokes. Promptly, ASAP, I mailed it back and waited. And waited. Another month passed. I wrote a letter of inquiry. At last came a note from a different editor—I believe his name was Mayer or Meyer—stating that my essay would not be printed because of "lack of space." No further explanation was offered. Nor did the letter enclose a check covering the customary kill fee. I sent the editors a bill for my time, trouble, and expenses, and asked for the return of my essay. This letter was not answered and my original copy never returned. Four years later *The New York Times* still owes me five hundred dollars plus eighty-eight cents in postage expenses.

Rejected by the *Times*, I mailed my immigration piece to other periodicals. In quick succession it was turned down by *Harper's*, *The Atlantic*, *The New Republic*, *Rolling Stone*, *Newsweek's* "My Turn" and—automatically—by *Mother Jones*. I should have known. Giving up on the national press, I persuaded Mike Lacey, editor of *New Times*, a Phoenix weekly, to publish my loathsome little essay in his magazine. Bravely, he agreed to do it, though covering himself by giving equal space for reply to a local Chicano politico. I did my part for interracial goodwill by donating my two-hundred-dollar fee to a Mexican-American arts center in Phoenix. The politico did his by calling me a racist. The only letters objecting to my piece came from middle-class whites, or "Anglos" as they are known in the American Southwest.

"Them there liberals," says my neighbor Dewey Foster, "they can't say the word *shit* even when their mouths is full of it." True fact, Dewey.

"Free Speech: The Cowboy and His Cow" began as notes for a speech written on an airplane flight between Tucson, Arizona, and Missoula, Montana, delivered next day under alcoholic conditions at the University of Montana before a rowdy crowd of five to six hundred students, ranchers, and instant rednecks (transplanted Easterners); it was reprinted verbatim, bawdy stories and all, in the Montana magazine *Northern Lights*. From there, much abridged but only slightly revised, this "speech" or "lecture" found its next home six months later in the pages of *Harper's* magazine. Unless I find something better to do, the piece may well conclude its career as the nucleus of a book-length essay in mythology and meat. The subject is a popular and hearty one. My treatment of it was rewarded by the usual blizzard of abuse, some seventy-five letters from outraged cattlepersons, including one Gretel Ehrlich of Shell, Wyoming (another instant redneck), who called me "arrogant, incoherent, flippant, nonsensical, nasty, and unconstructive . . ." A typical reaction: our cowgirls and beef ranchers are such *sensitive* people—touchier than lesbians, thin-skinned and high-strung as prima ballerinas.

("Nasty and unconstructive"—I love that.)

"A Writer's Credo" and "Emerson" were written as lectures, the first delivered at Harvard in May 1985 and again, somewhat expanded, at the 1986 conference of the Western Literature Association; the second as an introduction to a course in the American essay at the University of Arizona. These associations account for the pedantic tone; I was trying hard, on the three occasions, to appear sober, rational, respectable. I failed. But I tried.

"The Future of Sex" began as a routine book review for the *Bloomsbury Review* but escaped its ball and chain and took off for the territory ahead.

I am invited from time to time, as most writers are, to perform introductions to books by others: "Mr Krutch" appeared as a preface to a reissue of Krutch's *The Great Chain of Life*; "Blood Sport" as an introduction to Vance Bourjaily's charming work on bird-hunting, *The Unnatural Enemy*; "Eco-Defense" as a "forward!" to David Foreman's unique and essential book of the same title; "Wild Horses" as an introduction to the book *Wild Horses and Sacred Cows* by Richard Symanski.

What else? I wrote the long essay called "A San Francisco Journal" while employed for two weeks in the fall of 1986 as official writer-in-residence by the *San Francisco Examiner*, now one of the three or four best newspapers in the United States (the others being the L.A. *Times*, the *Chicago Sun-Times*, and of course the good gray magisterial *Moab Times-Independent* of Moab, Utah). Also, the *Examiner* pays its bills. "Theory of Anarchy" was written for *Earth First!: The Radical Environmental Journal* as a reply to criticism of anarchist folly by the historian Andrew Bard Schmookler. "Out There in the Rocks" I did as the script of a documentary for the NBC television show *Almanac*.

The remainder of the essays in this book are simple, straightforward travel pieces, no explanations necessary, written for and published in *The New York Times Magazine* ("Lake Powell by Houseboat"), *National Geographic* ("River of No Return," "Round River Rendezvous: The Rio Grande," "Forty Years as a Canyoneer," and "Big Bend"), a new periodical entitled *American Country* ("River Solitaire"), and *Architectural Digest* ("The Remington Studio").

"Arizona: How Big is Big Enough?" was a guest editorial for the *Arizona Daily Star*, Tucson.

My preliminary remarks leave one essay unaccounted for—"Sportsmen." This number, I confess, is a plagiarized paraphrase of what French critics (or Susan Sontag, who still hopes to grow up to be a Frenchman) might call *un enfant trouvé*—a lost objet d'art now found and restored in all the purity of its anonymous creation to the world of world literature, nature writing division. "Sportsmen," in this book or any to come, is my sole and final contribution to that venerable and ever-popular tradition.

Very well. If there's anyone still present whom I've failed to insult, I apologize.

Cheers!

> —*E. A.*
> *Oracle, Arizona*
> *May Day 1987*

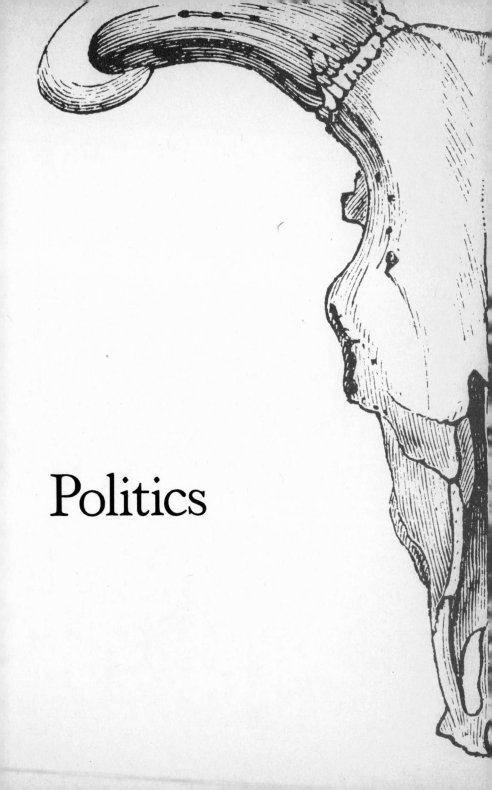

Politics

Free Speech

The Cowboy and His Cow

UNIVERSITY OF MONTANA, APRIL 1985

When I first came West in 1948, a student at the University of New Mexico, I was only twenty years old and just out of the Army. I thought, like most simple-minded Easterners, that a cowboy was a kind of mythic hero. I idolized those scrawny little red-nosed hired hands in their tight jeans, funny boots, and comical hats.

Like other new arrivals in the West, I could imagine nothing more romantic than becoming a cowboy. Nothing more glorious than owning my own little genuine working cattle outfit. About the only thing better, I thought, was to be a big-league baseball player. I never dreamed that I'd eventually sink to writing books for a living. Unluckily for me—coming from an Appalachian hillbilly background and with a poor choice of parents—I didn't have much money. My father was a small-time logger. He ran a one-man sawmill and a submarginal side-hill farm. There wasn't any money in our family, no inheritance you could run ten thousand cattle on. I had no trust fund to back me up. No Hollywood movie deals to finance a land acquisition program. I lived on what in those days was called the GI Bill, which paid about $150 a month while I went to school. I made that last as long as I could—five or six years. I couldn't afford a horse. The best I could do in 1947 and '48 was buy a third-hand Chevy sedan and roam the West, mostly the Southwest, on holidays and weekends.

I had a roommate at the University of New Mexico. I'll call him Mac. He came from a little town in southwest New Mexico where his father ran a feed store. Mackie was a fair bronc rider, eager to get into the cattle-growing business. And he had some money, enough to buy a little cinderblock house and about forty acres in the Sandia Mountains east of Albuquerque, near a town we called Landfill. Mackie fenced those forty acres, built a corral, and kept a few horses there, including an occasional genuine bronco for fun and practice.

I don't remember exactly how Mackie and I became friends in the first place. I was majoring in classical philosophy. He was majoring in screw-worm management. But we got to know each other through the mutual pursuit of a pair of nearly inseparable Kappa Kappa Gamma girls. I lived with him in his little cinderblock house. Helped him meet the mortgage payments. Helped him meet the girls. We were both crude, shy, ugly, obnoxious—like most college boys.

[*Interjection: "Like you!"*]

My friend Mac also owned a 1947 black Lincoln convertible, the kind with the big grille in front, like a cowcatcher on a locomotive, chrome-plated. We used to race to classes in the morning, driving the twenty miles from his house to the campus in never more than fifteen minutes. Usually Mac was too hung over to drive, so I'd operate the car, clutching the wheel while Mac sat beside me waving his big .44, taking potshots at jackrabbits and road signs and billboards and beer bottles. Trying to wake up in time for his ten o'clock class in brand inspection.

I'm sorry to say that my friend Mac was a little bit gun-happy.

[handwritten margin note: Some things never change]

Most of his forty acres was in tumbleweed. He fenced in about half an acre with chicken wire and stocked that little pasture with white rabbits. He used it as a target range. Not what you'd call sporting, I suppose, but we did eat the rabbits. Sometimes we even went deer hunting with handguns. Mackie with his revolver, and me with a chrome-plated Colt .45 automatic I had liberated from the US Army over in Italy. Surplus government property.

On one of our deer-hunting expeditions, I was sitting on a log in a big clearing in the woods, thinking about Plato and Aristotle and the Kappa Kappa Gamma girls. I didn't really care whether we got a deer that day or not. It was a couple of days before opening, anyway. The whole procedure was probably illegal as hell. Mac was out in the woods somewhere looking for deer around the clearing. I was sitting on the log, thinking, when I saw a chip of bark fly away from the log all by itself, about a foot from my left hand. Then I heard the blast of Mac's revolver—that big old .44 he'd probably liberated from his father. Then I heard him laugh.

"That's not very funny, Mackie," I said.

"Now don't whine and complain, Ed," he said. "You want to be a real hunter like me, you gotta learn to stay awake."

We never did get a deer with handguns. But that's when I had my first little doubts about Mackie, and about the cowboy type in general. But I still loved him. Worshipped him, in fact. I was caught in the grip of the Western myth. Anybody said a word to me against cowboys, I'd jump down his throat with my spurs on. Especially if Mac was standing nearby.

Sometimes I'd try to ride those broncs that he brought in, trying to prove that I could be a cowboy too. Trying to prove it more to myself than to him. I'd be on this crazy, crackpot horse going up, down, left, right, and inside out. Hanging on to the saddle horn with both hands. While Mac sat on the corral fence, throwing beer bottles at us and laughing. Every time I got thrown off, Mac would say, "Now get right back on there, Ed. Quick, quick. Don't spoil 'im."

It took me a long time to realize I didn't have to do that kind of work. And it took me another thirty years to realize that there's something wrong at the heart of our most popular American myth—the cowboy and his cow.

[*Jeers.*]

You may have guessed by now that I'm thinking of criticizing the livestock industry. And you are correct. I've been thinking about cows and sheep for many years. Getting more and more disgusted with the whole business. Western cattlemen are nothing more than welfare parasites. They've been getting a free ride on the public lands for over a century, and I think it's time we phased it out. I'm in favor of putting the public-lands livestock grazers out of business.

First of all, we don't need the public-lands beef industry. Even beef lovers don't need it. According to most government reports (Bureau of Land Management, Forest Service), only about 2 percent of our beef, our red meat, comes from the public lands of the eleven Western states. By those eleven I mean Montana, Nevada, Utah, Colorado, New Mexico, Arizona, Idaho, Wyoming, Oregon, Washington, and California. Most of our beef, aside from imports, comes from the Midwest and the East, especially the Southeast—Georgia, Alabama, Florida—and from other private lands across the nation. More beef cattle are raised in the state of Georgia than in the sagebrush empire of Nevada. And for a very good reason: back East, you can support a cow on maybe half an acre. Out here, it takes anywhere from twenty-five to fifty acres. In the red-rock country of Utah, the rule of thumb is one section—a square mile—per cow.

[*Shouts from rear of hall.*]

Since such a small percentage of cows are produced on public lands in the West, eliminating that part of the industry should not raise supermarket beef prices very much. Furthermore, we'd save money in the taxes we now pay for various subsidies to these public-lands cattlemen. Subsidies for things like "range improvement"—tree chaining, sagebrush clearing, mesquite poisoning, disease control, predator trapping, fencing, wells, stockponds, roads. Then there are the salaries of those who work for government agencies like the BLM and the Forest Service. You could probably also count in a big part of the salaries of the overpaid professors engaged in range-management research at the Western land-grant colleges.

Moreover, the cattle have done, and are doing, intolerable damage to our public lands—our national forests, state lands, BLM-administered lands, wildlife preserves, even some of our national parks and monuments. In Utah's Capital Reef National Park, for example, grazing is still allowed. In fact, it's recently been extended for another ten years, and Utah politicians are trying to make the arrangement permanent. They probably won't get away with it. But there we have at least one case where cattle are still tramping about in a national park, transforming soil and grass into dust and weeds.

[*Disturbance.*]

Overgrazing is much too weak a term. Most of the public lands in the West, and especially in the Southwest, are what you might call "cowburnt." Almost anywhere and everywhere you go in the American West you find hordes of these ugly, clumsy, stupid, bawling, stinking, fly-covered, shit-smeared, disease-spreading brutes. They are a pest and a plague. They pollute our springs and streams and rivers. They infest our canyons, valleys, meadows, and forests. They graze off the native bluestem and grama and bunch grasses, leaving behind jungles of prickly pear. They trample down the native forbs and shrubs and cacti. They spread the exotic cheatgrass, the Russian thistle, and the crested wheat grass. *Weeds*.

Even when the cattle are not physically present, you'll see the dung and the flies and the mud and the dust and the general destruction. If you don't see it, you'll smell it. The whole American West stinks of cattle. Along every flowing stream, around every seep and spring and water hole and well, you'll find acres and acres of what range-management specialists call "sacrifice areas"—another understatement. These are places denuded of forage, except for some cactus or a little tumbleweed or maybe a few mutilated trees like mesquite, juniper, or hackberry.

I'm not going to bombard you with graphs and statistics, which don't make much of an impression on intelligent people anyway. Anyone who goes beyond the city limits of almost any Western town can see for himself that the land is overgrazed. There are too many cows and horses and sheep out there. Of course, cattlemen would never publicly confess to overgrazing, any more than Dracula would publicly confess to a fondness for blood. Cattlemen are interested parties. Many of them will not give reliable testimony. Some have too much at stake: their Cadillacs and their airplanes, their ranch resale profits and their capital gains. (I'm talking about the corporation ranchers, the land-and-cattle companies, the investment syndicates.) Others, those ranchers who have only a small base property, flood the public lands with their cows. About 8 percent of the federal land permittees have cattle that consume approximately 45 percent of the forage on the government rangelands.

Beef ranchers like to claim that their cows do not compete with deer. Deer are browsers, cows are grazers. That's true. But when a range is overgrazed, when the grass is gone (as it often is for seasons at a time), then cattle become browsers too, out of necessity. In the Southwest, cattle commonly feed on mesquite, cliff rose, cactus, acacia, or any other shrub or tree they find biodegradable. To that extent, they compete with deer. And they tend to drive out other and better wildlife. Like elk, or bighorn sheep, or pronghorn antelope.

[*Sneers, jeers, laughter.*]

How much damage have cattle done to the Western rangelands? Large-scale beef ranching has been going on since the 1870s. There's plenty of documentation of the effects of this massive cattle grazing on the erosion of the land, the character of the land, the character of the vegetation. Streams and rivers that used to flow on the surface all year round are now intermittent, or underground, because of overgrazing and rapid runoff.

Our public lands have been overgrazed for a century. The BLM knows it; the Forest Service knows it. The Government Accounting Office knows it. And overgrazing means eventual ruin, just like stripmining or clear-cutting or the damming of rivers. Much of the Southwest already looks like Mexico or southern Italy or North Africa: a cowburnt wasteland. As we destroy our land, we destroy our agricultural economy and the basis of modern society. If we keep it up, we'll gradually degrade American life to the status of life in places like Mexico or southern Italy or Libya or Egypt.

In 1984 the Bureau of Land Management, which was required by Congress to report on its stewardship of our rangelands—the property of all Americans, remember—confessed that 31 percent of the land it administered was in "good condition," and 60 percent in "poor condition." And it reported that only 18 percent of the rangelands were improving, while 68 percent were "stable" and 14 percent were getting worse. If the BLM said that, we can safely assume that range conditions are actually much worse.

[*Shouts of "bullshit!"*]

What can we do about this situation? This is the fun part—this is the part I like. It's not easy to argue that we should do away with cattle ranching. The cowboy myth gets in the way. But I do have some solutions to overgrazing.

[*A yell: "Cowboys do it better!" Answered by another: "Ask any cow!" Coarse laughter.*]

I'd begin by reducing the number of cattle on public lands. Not that range managers would go along with it, of course. In their eyes, and in the eyes of the livestock associations they work for, cutting down on the number of cattle is the worst possible solution—an impossible solution. So they propose all kinds of gimmicks. Portable fencing and perpetual movement of cattle. More cross-fencing. More wells and ponds so that more land can be exploited. These proposals are basically a maneuver by the Forest Service and the BLM to appease their critics without offending their real bosses in the beef industry. But a drastic reduction in cattle numbers is the only true and honest solution.

I also suggest that we open a hunting season on range cattle. I realize that beef cattle will not make sporting prey at first. Like all domesticated animals (including most humans), beef cattle are slow, stupid, and awkward. But the breed will improve if hunted regularly. And as the number of cattle is reduced, other and far more useful, beautiful, and interesting animals will return to the rangelands and will increase.

Suppose, by some miracle of Hollywood or inheritance or good luck, I should acquire a respectable-sized working cattle outfit. What would I do with it? First, I'd get rid of the stinking, filthy cattle. Every single animal. Shoot them all, and stock the place with real animals, real game, real protein: elk, buffalo, pronghorn antelope, bighorn sheep, moose. And some purely decorative animals, like eagles. We need more eagles. And wolves. We need more wolves. Mountain lions and bears. Especially, of course, grizzly bears. Down in the desert, I would stock every water tank, every water hole, every stockpond, with alligators.

You may note that I have said little about coyotes or deer. Coyotes seem to be doing all right on their own. They're smarter than their enemies. I've never heard of a coyote as dumb as a sheepman. As for deer, especially mule deer, they, too, are surviving—maybe even thriving, as some game and fish departments claim, though nobody claims there are as many deer now as there were before the cattle industry was introduced in the West. In any case, compared to elk the deer is a second-rate game animal, nothing but a giant rodent—a rat with antlers.

[*Portions of audience begin to leave.*]

I've suggested that the beef industry's abuse of our Western lands is based on the old mythology of the cowboy as natural nobleman. I'd like to conclude this diatribe with a few remarks about this most cherished and fanciful of American fairy tales. In truth, the cowboy is only a hired hand. A farm boy in leather britches and a comical hat. A herdsman who gets on a horse to do part of his work. Some ranchers are also cowboys, but most are not. There is a difference. There are many ranchers out there who are big-time farmers of the public lands—our property. As such, they do not merit any special consideration or special privileges. There are only about 31,000 ranchers in the whole American West who use the public lands. That's less than the population of Missoula, Montana.

The rancher (with a few honorable exceptions) is a man who strings barbed wire all over the range; drills wells and bulldozes stockponds; drives off elk and antelope and bighorn sheep; poisons coyotes and prairie dogs; shoots eagles, bears, and cougars on sight; supplants the native grasses with tumbleweed, snakeweed, povertyweed, cowshit, anthills, mud, dust, and flies. And then leans back and grins at the TV cameras and talks about how much he loves the American West. Cowboys also are greatly overrated. Consider the nature of their work. Suppose you had to spend most of your working hours sitting on a horse, contemplating the hind end of a cow. How would that affect your imagination? Think what it does to the relatively simple mind of the average peasant boy, raised amid the bawling of calves and cows in the splatter of mud and the stink of shit.

[*Shouting. Laughter. Disturbance.*]

Do cowboys work hard? Sometimes. But most ranchers don't work very hard. They have a lot of leisure time for politics and bellyaching (which is why most state legislatures in the West are occupied and dominated by cattlemen). Anytime you go into a small Western town you'll find them at the nearest drugstore, sitting around all morning drinking coffee, talking about their tax breaks.

Is a cowboy's work socially useful? No. As I've already pointed out, subsidized Western range beef is a trivial item in the national beef economy. If all of our 31,000 Western public-land ranchers quit tomorrow, we'd never even notice. Any public school teacher does harder work, more difficult work, more dangerous work, and far more valuable work than the cowboy or rancher. The same thing applies to registered nurses and nurses' aides, garbage collectors, and traffic cops. Harder work, tougher work, more necessary work. We need those people in our complicated society. We do not need cowboys or ranchers. We've carried them on our backs long enough.

[*Disturbance in rear of hall.*]

"This Abbey," the cowboys and their lovers will say, "this Abbey is a wimp. A chicken-hearted sentimentalist with no feel for the hard realities of practical life." Especially critical of my attitude will be the Easterners and Midwesterners newly arrived here from their Upper West Side apartments, their rustic lodges in upper Michigan. Our nouveau Westerners with their toy ranches, their pickup trucks with the gun racks, their pointy-toed boots with the undershot heels, their gigantic hats. And, of course, their pet horses. The *instant rednecks*.

[*Shouts.*]

To those who might accuse me of wimpery and sentimentality, I'd like to say this in reply. I respect real men. I admire true manliness. But I despise arrogance and brutality and bullies. So let me close with some nice remarks about cowboys and cattle ranchers. They are a mixed lot, like the rest of us. As individuals, they range from the bad to the ordinary to the good. A rancher, after all, is only a farmer, cropping the public rangelands with his four-legged lawnmowers, stashing our grass into his bank account. A cowboy is a hired hand trying to make an honest living. Nothing special.

I have no quarrel with these people as fellow humans. All I want to do is get their cows off our property. Let those cowboys and ranchers find some harder way to make a living, like the rest of us have to do. There's no good reason why we should subsidize them forever. They've had their free ride. It's time they learned to support themselves.

In the meantime, I'm going to say good-bye to all you cowboys and cowgirls. I love the legend too—but keep your sacred cows and your dead horses out of my elk pastures.

[*Sitting ovation. Gunfire in parking lot.*]

Arizona

How Big is Big Enough?

Governor Bruce Babbitt tells us that by the year 2000, only sixteen years from now, Arizona will gain two million new residents, that Phoenix will become another Houston and Tucson another Phoenix, and that we will have an additional one million automobiles crowding our streets and highways. Tucson Mayor Lew Murphy—unable to conceal his smirking glee—predicts that Tucson will become, within twenty years, a 450-square-mile urbanized area. Most of our reigning bankers, economists, and developers keep shelling us with a similar barrage of thundering numbers. This, our leaders tell us, is good news. Growth is good, they say, reciting like an incantation the prime article of faith of the official American religion: Bigger is better and best is biggest. Growth, they tell us, means more jobs, more bank accounts, more cars, more people, leading in turn to the demand for more jobs, more economic expansion, more industrial development. Where, when, and how is this spiraling process supposed to reach a rational end—a state of stability, sanity, and equilibrium?

When and if Arizona becomes like Southern California or South Central Texas or the Baltimore-to-Boston megalopolis, will people like Murphy and Babbitt and the corporation executives from whom they take their instructions then be satisfied? Or will our children be faced, once again, with new and greater demands for still more growth?

Already looking beyond the completion of the Central Arizona Project, Babbitt speaks of mining the ground water of Western Arizona. For what purpose? Why, to provide the essential liquid element for further growth. And when that supply is played out, as it is already playing out in Southern Arizona and the high plains of Texas, then what? The answer is easy to foresee: A great clamor from our Southwestern politicians to desalinate the Sea of Cortez, to import icebergs from Antarctica, to divert first the Columbia and then the Yukon rivers into the drainages of the Colorado.

Viewing it in this way, we can see that the religion of endless growth—like any religion based on blind faith rather than reason—is a kind of mania, a form of lunacy, indeed a disease. And the one disease to which the growth mania bears an exact analogical resemblance is cancer. Growth for the sake of growth is the ideology of the cancer cell. Cancer has no purpose but growth; but it does have another result—the death of the host.

But all this is mere futurology, like astrology and computerology and technology, only one of the many commercialized superstitions of our time. We need not look years ahead but simply look at the present to weigh the comparative advantages and disadvantages of industrial growth. We need only consider Phoenix and Tucson and decide which of the two is the more attractive, which is the better place to live in, make a living in, raise a family in.

It should be clear to everyone by now that crude numerical growth does not solve our chronic problems of unemployment, welfare, crime, traffic, filth, noise, squalor, the pollution of our air, the poisoning of our water, the corruption of our politics, the debasement of the school system (hardly worthy of the name "education"), and the general loss of popular control over the political process—where money, not people, is now the determining factor.

Far from solving such problems, industrial expansion and population growth only make them worse. Does Houston really provide us with a model to aspire toward? Or Chicago? New York? Los Angeles? Miami? Or maybe Mexico City?

Ah well, say our alleged leaders, in response to this sort of argument, we face a challenge. Our politicians love that word. And the challenge, they tell us, is to accommodate ourselves to endless growth without sacrificing the quality of the Arizona environment, without losing the bright skies, the bracing air, the open space, the abundant wildlife, the desert plant life, the sheer delight of physical freedom, all of those good and unique and irreplaceable things that are in sum what attracted most of us to Arizona in the first place.

We can have it both ways, they say. We can enjoy our cake and at the same time destroy it, grind it to bits in the urbanizing, industrializing mill, and transform what we prize into boom time if temporary, jobs for thousands and fat bank accounts for the tiny but powerful minority of land speculators, tract-slum builders, bankers, car dealers, and shopping-mall hustlers who stand to profit from what they call growth.

This argument hardly requires an answer. The so-called challenge is a plain lie. All industrial development involves a trade-off: in order to make room for more growth, we must give up the very qualities that make a high standard of civilized human life still possible in Arizona—as contrasted to, say, the frantic, crowded, substandard life of California's Silicon Valley. (Do you really want to live in a place where the microchip is the highest object of human desire?)

And now we come to the final argument of growth zealots. Growth, they say, is inevitable. There is nothing, they say, that we can do about it. There is no constitutional means by which we can prevent two million more flatlanders from invading Arizona in the next sixteen years.

This is the baldest lie of them all. Nothing is inevitable but death, taxes, and the insolent dishonesty (as Mark Twain said) of elected officials.

The fact is that the fungoid growth of Arizona in recent years has been the result of deliberate policy. The only purpose of the CAP is to make possible the continued growth of Central and Southern Arizona. The same is true of the Palo Verde nuclear power plant and the various new coal-burning plants now polluting the public air.

The only purpose of the state's pro-business, anti-labor position is to lure industry here—and if this policy causes misery and hardship elsewhere, that is of no concern to our leaders. The only purpose of freeway projects, highway building, river-damming, pro-development rezoning, and opposition to wilderness preservation, naming but a few measures, is to make possible, encourage, and create the runaway growth that enriches a few and gradually impoverishes the rest of us.

If we in Arizona did our part in keeping American industry where it now is, we would also help keep Arizona what it is. People follow industry, high-technology or otherwise, not because they enjoy being uprooted from their homes but out of painful economic need.

Does my attitude seem selfish? Of course it is. I have lived in the Southwest since 1947—forty years—most of my life. During most of those years, I survived on part-time work and the precarious existence of a free-lance writer, usually on an income below the official US government poverty line. I did it because I love Arizona and the Southwest, preferably as it was but even as it is. And because I love it, I do not want to see our state become one more high-tech slum like California or a wasteland of space-age sleaze like Texas. I have a sneaking suspicion there's about a million other Arizonans who feel the same way I do.

We cannot creep from quantity to quality. It's high time we told the little cabal who run this state that Tucson is big enough, Phoenix is big enough, Arizona is big enough. What we need is not more growth but more democracy—and democracy, some other old-timers may recall, means government by the people. *By* the people.

Theory of Anarchy

*T*he Bible says that the love of money is the root of all evil. But what is the essential meaning of money? Money attracts because it gives us the means to command the labor and service and finally the lives of others—human or otherwise. Money is power. I would expand the Biblical aphorism, therefore, in this fashion: the root of all evil is the love of power.

And power attracts the worst and corrupts the best among men. It is no accident that police work, for example, appeals to those (if not only those) with the bully's instinct. We know the type. Or put a captain's bars on a perfectly ordinary, decent man, give him a measure of arbitrary power over others, and he tends to become—unless a man of unusual character—a martinet, another petty despot. Power corrupts; and as Lord Acton pointed out, absolute power corrupts absolutely. The problem of democracy is the problem of power—how to keep power decentralized, equally distributed, fairly shared. Anarchism means maximum democracy: the maximum possible dispersal of political power, economic power, and force—military power. An anarchist society consists of a voluntary association of self-reliant, self-supporting, autonomous communities. The anarchist community would consist (as it did in preagricultural and preindustrial times) of a voluntary association of free and independent families, self-reliant and self-supporting but bound by kinship ties and a tradition of mutual aid.

Anarchy is democracy taken seriously, as in Switzerland, where issues of national importance are decided by direct vote of all citizens. Where each citizen, after his period of military training, takes his weapon home with him, to keep for life. Anarchy is democracy taken all the way, in every major sector of social life. For example, political democracy will not survive in a society which permits a few to accumulate economic power over the many. Or in a society which delegates police power and military power to an elite corps of professionals. Sooner or later the professionals will take over. In my notion of an anarchist community every citizen—man or woman—would be armed, trained, capable when necessary of playing the part of policeman or soldier. A healthy community polices itself; a healthy society would do the same. Looters, thugs, criminals, may appear anywhere, anytime, but in nature such types are mutants, anomalies, a minority; the members of a truly democratic, anarchistic community would not require outside assistance in dealing with them. Some might call this vigilante justice; I call it democratic justice. Better to have all citizens participate in the suppression and punishment of crime—and share in the moral responsibility—than turn the nasty job over to some quasi-criminal type (or hero) in a uniform with a tin badge on his shirt. Yes, we need heroes. We need heroines. But they should serve only as inspiration and examples, not as leaders.

No doubt the people of today's Lebanon, for example, would settle gladly for an authoritarian government capable of suppressing the warring factions. But such an authoritarian government would provoke the return of the irrepressible human desire for freedom, leading in turn to rebellion, revolt, and revolution. If Lebanon were not so badly overpopulated, the best solution there—as in South Africa—would be a partition of territory, a devolution into self-governing, independent regions and societies. This is the natural tendency of any population divided by religion, race, or deep cultural differences, and it should not be restrained. The tendency runs counter, however, to the love of power, which is why centralized governments always attempt to crush separatist movements.

Government is a social machine whose function is coercion through monopoly of power. Any good Marxist understands this. Like a bulldozer, government serves the caprice of any man or group who succeeds in seizing the controls. The purpose of anarchism is to dismantle such institutions and to prevent their reconstruction. Ten thousand years of human history demonstrate that our freedoms cannot be entrusted to those ambitious few who are drawn to power; we must learn—again—to govern ourselves. Anarchism does not mean "no rule"; it means "no rulers." Difficult but not utopian, anarchy means and requires self-rule, self-discipline, probity, character.

At present, life in America is far better for the majority than in most (not all) other nations. But that fact does not excuse our failings. Judged by its resources, intentions, and potential, the great American experiment appears to me as a failure. We have not become the society of independent freeholders that Jefferson envisioned; nor have we evolved into a true democracy—government *by* the people—as Lincoln imagined.

Instead we see the realization of the scheme devised by Madison and Hamilton: a strong centralized state which promotes and protects the accumulation of private wealth on the part of a few, while reducing the majority to the role of dependent employees of state and industry. We are a nation of helots ruled by an oligarchy of techno-military-industrial administrators.

Never before in history have slaves been so well fed, thoroughly medicated, lavishly entertained—but we are slaves nonetheless. Our debased popular culture—television, rock music, home video, processed food, mechanical recreation, wallboard architecture—is the culture of slaves. Furthermore the whole grandiose structure is self-destructive: by enshrining the profit motive (power) as our guiding ideal, we encourage the intensive and accelerating consumption of land, air, water— the natural world—on which the structure depends for its continued existence. A house built on greed will not long endure. Whether it's called capitalism or socialism makes little difference; both of these oligarchic, militaristic, expansionist, acquisitive, industrializing, and technocratic systems are driven by the same motives; both are self-destroying. Even without the accident of a nuclear war, I predict that the military-industrial state will disappear from the surface of the earth within a century. That belief is the basis of my inherent optimism, the source of my hope for the coming restoration of a higher civilization: scattered human populations modest in number that live by fishing, hunting, food gathering, small-scale farming and ranching, that gather once a year in the ruins of abandoned cities for great festivals of moral, spiritual, artistic, and intellectual renewal, a people for whom the wilderness is not a playground but their natural native home.

New dynasties will arise, new tyrants will appear—no doubt. But we must and we can resist such recurrent aberrations by keeping true to the earth and remaining loyal to our basic animal nature. Humans were free before the word *freedom* became necessary. Slavery is a cultural invention. Liberty is life: *eros* plus *anarchos* equals *bios*.

Long live democracy.

Two cheers for anarchy.

Eco-Defense

*I*f a stranger batters your
door down with an axe, threatens your family and yourself with
deadly weapons, and proceeds to loot your home of whatever
he wants, he is committing what is universally recognized—by
law and in common morality—as a crime. In such a situation
the householder has both the right and the obligation to defend
himself, his family, and his property by whatever means are
necessary. This right and this obligation is universally recognized, justified, and praised by all civilized human communities. Self-defense against attack is one of the basic laws not only
of human society but of life itself, not only of human life but
of all life.

The American wilderness, what little remains, is now
undergoing exactly such an assault. With bulldozer, earth mover,
chainsaw, and dynamite the international timber, mining, and
beef industries are invading our public lands—property of all
Americans—bashing their way into our forests, mountains, and
rangelands and looting them for everything they can get away

with. This for the sake of short-term profits in the corporate sector and multimillion-dollar annual salaries for the three-piece-suited gangsters (MBA—Harvard, Yale, University of Tokyo, et alia) who control and manage these bandit enterprises. Cheered on, naturally, by *Time*, *Newsweek*, and *The Wall Street Journal*, actively encouraged, inevitably, by those jellyfish government agencies that are supposed to *protect* the public lands, and as always aided and abetted in every way possible by the compliant politicians of our Western states, such as Babbitt, DeConcini, Goldwater, McCain, Hatch, Garn, Simms, Hansen, Andrus, Wallop, Domenici and Co. Inc.—who would sell the graves of their mothers if there's a quick buck in the deal, over or under the table, what do they care.

Representative government in the United States has broken down. Our legislators do not represent the public, the voters, or even those who voted for them but rather the commercial-industrial interests that finance their political campaigns and control the organs of communication—the TV, the newspapers, the billboards, the radio. Politics is a game for the rich only. Representative government in the USA represents money, not people, and therefore has forfeited our allegiance and moral support. We owe it nothing but the taxation it extorts from us under threats of seizure of property, imprisonment, or in some cases already, when resisted, a violent death by gunfire.

Such is the nature and structure of the industrial megamachine (in Lewis Mumford's term) which is now attacking the American wilderness. That wilderness is our ancestral home, the primordial homeland of all living creatures including the human, and the present final dwelling place of such noble beings as the grizzly bear, the mountain lion, the eagle and the condor, the moose and the elk and the pronghorn antelope, the redwood tree, the yellow pine, the bristlecone pine, and yes, why not say it?—the streams, waterfalls, rivers, the very bedrock itself of our hills, canyons, deserts, mountains. For many of us, perhaps for most of us, the wilderness is more our home than the little stucco boxes, wallboard apartments, plywood trailer-houses, and cinderblock condominiums in which the majority are now confined by the poverty of an overcrowded industrial culture.

And if the wilderness is our true home, and if it is threatened with invasion, pillage, and destruction—as it certainly is—then we have the right to defend that home, as we would our private quarters, by whatever means are necessary. (An Englishman's home is his castle; the American's home is his favorite forest, river, fishing stream, her favorite mountain or desert canyon, his favorite swamp or woods or lake.) We have the right to resist and we have the obligation; not to defend that which we love would be dishonorable. The majority of the American people have demonstrated on every possible occasion that they support the ideal of wilderness preservation; even our politicians are forced by popular opinion to *pretend* to support the idea; as they have learned, a vote against wilderness is a vote against their own reelection. We are justified then in defending our homes—our private home and our public home—not only by common law and common morality but also by common belief. We are the majority; they—the powerful—are in the minority.

How best defend our homes? Well, that is a matter of the strategy, tactics, and technique which eco-defense is all about.

What is eco-defense? Eco-defense means fighting back. Eco-defense means sabotage. Eco-defense is risky but sporting; unauthorized but fun; illegal but ethically imperative. Next time you enter a public forest scheduled for chainsaw massacre by some timber corporation and its flunkies in the US Forest Service, carry a hammer and a few pounds of 60-penny nails in your creel, saddlebag, game bag, backpack, or picnic basket.

Spike those trees; you won't hurt them; they'll be grateful for the protection; and you may save the forest. Loggers hate nails. My Aunt Emma back in West Virginia has been enjoying this pleasant exercise for years. She swears by it. It's good for the trees, it's good for the woods, and it's good for the human soul. Spread the word.

Blood Sport

What can I say about hunting that hasn't been said before? Hunting is one of the hardest things even to think about. Such a storm of conflicting emotions!

I was born, bred, and raised on a farm in the Allegheny Mountains of Pennsylvania. A little sidehill farm in hardscrabble country, a land of marginal general farms, of submarginal specialized farms—our specialty was finding enough to eat without the shame of going on "The Relief," as we called it during the Great Depression of the 1930s. We lived in the hills, surrounded by scrubby third-growth forests, little coal-mining towns down in the valleys, and sulfur-colored creeks meandering among the corn patches. Few people could make a living from farming alone: my father, for example, supplemented what little we produced on the farm by occasional work in the mines, by driving a school bus, by a one-man logging business, by peddling subscriptions to a farmer's magazine, and by attending every private and public shooting match within fifty miles of home—he was an expert small-bore rifleman and a member, for several years running, of the Pennsylvania state rifle team; he still has a sashful of medals to show for those years. He almost always brought back from the matches a couple of chickens, sometimes a turkey, once a yearling pig.

None of this was quite enough, all together, to keep a family of seven in meat, all the time, through the frozen Appalachian winters. So he hunted. We all hunted. All of our neighbors hunted. Nearly every boy I knew had his own rifle, and maybe a shotgun too, by the time he was twelve years old. As I did myself.

What did we hunt? Cottontail rabbit, first and foremost; we'd kill them, clean them, skin them, cut them up; my mother deep-fried them in bread crumbs and cooked and canned the surplus in Mason jars, as she did tomatoes, stringbeans, succotash, pork sausage, peaches, pears, sweet corn, everything else that would keep. We had no deep-freeze; in fact, we had no electricity until the Rural Electrification Administration reached our neck of the woods in 1940.

So rabbit was almost a staple of our diet; fencerow chicken, we called it, as good and familiar to us as henyard chicken. My father seldom bothered with squirrel, but my brothers and I potted a few with our little Sears Roebuck single-shot .22s, out among the great ancient white oaks and red oaks that were still standing in our woodlot. Squirrel meat can be good, but not so good as rabbit, and a squirrel is much harder to kill; we missed about ten for every one we hit.

There were no wild ducks or other waterfowl in the hills; our only gamebird was the ringneck pheasant, rising with a thrilling rush from the corn stubble. My father bagged a few of those with his old taped-together double-barrel shotgun. Not many. He didn't like to hunt with a shotgun. Wasteful, he thought, and the shells were too expensive, and besides, he disliked chewing on lead pellets. The shotgun was primarily a weapon (though never needed) for home defense. Most of the time he shot rabbits with his target rifle, a massive magazine-loaded .22 with a peep sight. Shot them sitting.

Was that legal? Probably. I don't remember. But he had a good eye. And he was a hunter—not a sportsman. He hunted for a purpose: to put meat on the table.

We kept a couple of beagle hounds on the place, but their job was to lie under the front porch and bark at strangers. Only when our Uncle Jack came out from town, with his sleek gleaming 16-gauge pumpgun (as we called it), and the red bandana and hunting license pinned to the back of his hunting coat, only then would our old man load his own shotgun and turn loose the dogs for some sport hunting through the fields and along the edge of the woods. What my father really liked about those occasions was not the shooting but the talk, the wild stories— Uncle Jack was a great storyteller.

And then there were the deer. The woods of Pennsylvania swarmed with deer, though not so many then as now, when many small farms, abandoned, have gone back to brush, thicket, trees. There were even a few black bear still wandering the woods, rarely seen. But deer was the principal game.

My father usually bought a license for deer, when he could afford it, but only because the penalty for getting caught with an untagged deer would have been a small financial catastrophe. In any case, with or without a license, he always killed his deer on the evening before opening day, while those red-coated fellows from the towns and cities were busy setting up their elaborate camps along the back roads, stirring the deer into movement. Our father was not a stickler for strict legality, and he believed, as most country men did, that fear tainted the meat and therefore it was better to get your deer before the chase, the gunnery—The Terror—began. We liked our venison poached. (As a result I find that after these many years I retain more admiration and respect for the honest serious poacher than I do or ever could for the so-called "gentleman hunter.")

My old man practiced what we called "still hunting." On the day before opening, about noon, when the deer were bedded down for their midday siesta, he'd go out with his gun, his cornfodder-tan canvas coat with its many big pockets, and his coal miner's oval-shaped lunch bucket full of hot coffee and sandwiches and Mother's stewed-raisin cookies, and he'd pick a familiar spot along one of the half-dozen game paths in our neighborhood, settle down in the brush with his back to a comfortable tree, and wait. And keep on waiting, sometimes into the long autumn twilight, until at last the first somewhat nervous, always uneasy deer appeared. Doe or buck, he always shot whatever came first. You can't eat antlers, he pointed out.

Usually he shot his deer with a "punkin ball" from the battered, dangerous, taped-up shotgun. But at least once, as I recall, he dropped a doe with his target rifle, like a rabbit. Drilled her right between the eyes with a neat little .22-caliber long-rifle bullet. Those deer slugs for the shotgun were expensive.

Then he'd drag the deer into the brush, out of sight, and wait some more, to see if anyone had noticed the shot. When nothing happened, he hung the deer to the nearest tree limb, dressed it out, ate the liver for supper. If it was a legal kill he would wait through the night, tag it, and take it home by wheel first thing in the morning. If not, he slung the carcass over his shoulders and toted it home through the woods and over the hills in the dark. He was a strong, large, and resolute sort of man then, back in the thirties and early forties, with a wife and five children to feed. Nowadays, getting on a bit—he was born in 1901—he is still oversize, for an old man, but not so strong physically. Nor so resolute. He works only four or five hours a day, alone, out in the woods, cutting down trees, and then quits. He gave up deer hunting thirty years ago.

Why? "Well," he explains, "we don't need the meat any more."

Now that was how my brothers and I learned about hunting. My brothers still like to go out for deer now and then, but it's road hunting, with good companions, not "still hunting." I wonder if anybody hunts in that fashion these days. I did a lot of deer hunting in New Mexico from 1947 through the 1950s, during my student years and later, when I was living on seasonal jobs with the Park Service and Forest Service, often married, trying to write books. As my father had taught me, I usually went out on the day before opening. Much safer then, for one thing, before those orange-vested hordes were turned loose over the landscape, shooting at everything that moves.

Gradually, from year to year, my interest in hunting, as a sport, waned away to nothing. I began to realize that what I liked best about hunting was the companionship of a few good old trusted male buddies in the out-of-doors. Anything, any excuse, to get out into the hills, away from the crowds, to live, if only for a few days, beyond the wall. That was the point of hunting.

So why lug a ten-pound gun along? I began leaving my rifle in the truck. Then I left it at home. The last time I looked down the bore of that old piece there was a spider living there.

"We don't need the meat any more," says my old man. And I say, Let the mountain lions have those deer; they need the meat more than I do. Let the Indians have it, or hungry college students, or unpublished writers, or anyone else trying to get by on welfare, food stamps, and hope. When the money began arriving from New York by airmail, those checks with my name on them, like manna from heaven, I gave up hunting deer. I had no need. Every time you eat a cow, I tell myself, you are saving the life of an elk, or two mule deer, or about two dozen javelina. Let those wild creatures live. Let being be, said Martin Heidegger. Of course, they're going to perish anyway, I know, whether by lion or wolf or starvation or disease—but so are we. We are all going to perish, and most of us miserably, by war or in a hospital, unless we are very lucky. Or very resolute. I am aware of that fact and of our fate, and furthermore, I have no objections to it, none whatsoever. I fear pain, suffering, the likely humiliations of old age (unless I am lucky or resolute), but I do not fear death. Death is simply and obviously a part of the process; the old, sooner or later, have got to get out of the way and make room for the young.

The subject remains: death. Blood sport. The instinct to hunt. The desire to kill. Henry David Thoreau, notorious nature lover, was also a hunter and fisherman, on occasion. And among the many things that Thoreau wrote on the matter was this, from *Walden*:

There is a period in the history of the individual, as of the race, when the hunters are the "best men," as the Algonquins called them. We cannot but pity the boy who has never fired a gun; he is no more humane, while his education has been sadly neglected.

But he adds:

No humane being, past the thoughtless age of boyhood, will wantonly murder any creature which holds its life by the same tenure he does. The hare in its extremity cries like a child. I warn you, mothers, that my sympathies do not make the usual *philanthropic* distinctions.

And concludes:

> But I see that if I were to live in a wilderness, I should
> become . . . a fisher and hunter in earnest.

In earnest. There lies the key to the ethical issue. Earnestness.
Purpose. That sly sophist Ortega y Gasset wrote, somewhere,
that "one kills in order to have hunted." Not good enough.
Thoreau would say, one kills in order to eat. The killing is
justified by the need and must be done in a spirit of respect,
reverence, gratitude. Otherwise hunting sinks to the level of
mere fun, "harvesting animals," *divertissement*, sadism, or sport.
Sport!

Where did the ugly term "harvesting" come from? To speak
of "harvesting" other living creatures, whether deer or elk or
birds or cottontail rabbits, as if they were no more than a crop,
exposes the meanest, cruelest, most narrow and homocentric
of possible human attitudes toward the life that surrounds us.
The word reveals the pervasive influence of utilitarian economics in the modern mindset; and of all the sciences, economics
is the most crude and obtuse as well as dismal. Such doctrine
insults and violates both humanity and life; and humanity will
be, already is, the victim of it.

Now I have railed against the sportsman hunter long enough.
I wished only to explain why first my father and then I have
given up hunting, for the time being. When times get hard
again, as they surely will, when my family and kin need meat
on the table, I shall not hesitate to take that old carbine down
from the wall and ramrod that spider out of the barrel and
wander back once more into the hills.

"Paw," says my little brother, as the old man loads the shotgun,
"let me shoot the deer this time."

"You shut up," I say.

Our father smiles. "Quiet," he whispers, "both of you. Maybe next year." He peers down the dim path in the woods, into the gathering evening. "Be real still now. They're a-comin'. And Ned—" He squeezes my shoulder. "You hold that light on 'em good and steady this time."

"Yes, sir," I whisper back. "Sure will, Paw."

Immigration and
Liberal Taboos

*I*n the American South-
west, where I happen to live, only sixty miles north of the
Mexican border, the subject of illegal aliens is a touchy one—
almost untouchable. Even the terminology is dangerous: the
old word *wetback* is now considered a racist insult by all good
liberals; and the perfectly correct terms *illegal alien* and *illegal
immigrant* can set off charges of xenophobia, elitism, fascism,
and the ever-popular genocide against anyone careless enough
to use them. The only acceptable euphemism, it now appears,
is something called *undocumented worker*. Thus the pregnant
Mexican woman who appears, in the final stages of labor, at
the doors of the emergency ward of an El Paso or San Diego
hospital, demanding care for herself and the child she's about
to deliver, becomes an "undocumented worker." The child becomes an automatic American citizen by virtue of its place of
birth, eligible at once for all of the usual public welfare benefits.
And with the child comes not only the mother but the child's
family. And the mother's family. And the father's family. Can't

break up families, can we? They come to stay and they stay to multiply.

What of it? say the documented liberals; ours is a rich and generous nation, we have room for all, let them come. And let them stay, say the conservatives; a large, cheap, frightened, docile, surplus labor force is exactly what the economy needs. Put some fear into the unions: tighten discipline, spur productivity, whip up the competition for jobs. The conservatives love their cheap labor; the liberals love their cheap cause. (Neither group, you will notice, ever invites the immigrants to move into their *homes*. Not into *their* homes!) Both factions are supported by the cornucopia economists of the ever-expanding economy, who actually continue to believe that our basic resource is not land, air, water, but human bodies, more and more of them, the more the better in hive upon hive, world without end—ignoring the clear fact that those nations which most avidly practice this belief, such as Haiti, Puerto Rico, Mexico, to name only three, don't seem to be doing well. They look more like explosive slow-motion disasters, in fact, volcanic anthills, than functioning human societies. But that which our academic economists will not see and will not acknowledge is painfully obvious to *los latinos:* they stream north in ever-growing numbers.

Meanwhile, here at home in the land of endless plenty, we seem still unable to solve our traditional and nagging difficulties. After forty years of the most fantastic economic growth in the history of mankind, the United States remains burdened with mass unemployment, permanent poverty, an overloaded welfare system, violent crime, clogged courts, jam-packed prisons, commercial ("white-collar") crime, rotting cities and a poisoned environment, eroding farmlands and the disappearing family farm, all of the usual forms of racial, ethnic, and sexual conflict (which immigration further intensifies), plus the ongoing destruction of what remains of our forests, fields, mountains, lakes, rivers, and seashores, accompanied by the extermination of whole species of plants and animals. To name but a few of our little nagging difficulties.

This being so, it occurs to some of us that perhaps ever-continuing industrial and population growth is *not* the true road to human happiness, that simple gross quantitative increase of this kind creates only more pain, dislocation, confusion, and misery. In which case it might be wise for us as American citizens to consider calling a halt to the mass influx of even more millions of hungry, ignorant, unskilled, and culturally-morally-generically impoverished people. At least until we have brought our own affairs into order. Especially when these un-invited millions bring with them an alien mode of life which— let us be honest about this—is not appealing to the majority of Americans. Why not? Because we prefer democratic govern-ment, for one thing; because we still hope for an open, spacious, uncrowded, and beautiful—yes, beautiful!—society, for an-other. The alternative, in the squalor, cruelty, and corruption of Latin America, is plain for all to see.

Yes, I know, if the American Indians had enforced such a policy none of us pale-faced honkies would be here. But the Indians were foolish, and divided, and failed to keep our WASP ancestors out. They've regretted it ever since.

To everything there is a season, to every wave a limit, to every range an optimum capacity. The United States has been fully settled, and more than full, for at least a century. We have nothing to gain, and everything to lose, by allowing the old boat to be swamped. How many of us, truthfully, would *prefer* to be submerged in the Caribbean-Latin version of civilization? (Howls of "Racism! Elitism! Xenophobia!" from the Marx broth-ers and the documented liberals.) Harsh words: but somebody has to say them. We cannot play "let's pretend" much longer, not in the present world.

Therefore—let us close our national borders to any further

mass immigration, legal or illegal, from any source, as does every other nation on earth. The means are available, it's a simple technical-military problem. Even our Pentagon should be able to handle it. We've got an army somewhere on this planet, let's bring our soldiers home and station them where they can be of some actual and immediate benefit to the taxpayers who support them. That done, we can begin to concentrate attention on badly neglected internal affairs. *Our* internal affairs. Everyone would benefit, including the neighbors. Especially the neighbors.

Ah yes. But what *about* those hungry hundreds of millions, those anxious billions, yearning toward the United States from every dark and desperate corner of the world? Shall we simply ignore them? Reject them? Is such a course possible?

"Poverty," said Samuel Johnson, "is the great enemy of human happiness. It certainly destroys liberty, makes some virtues impracticable, and all virtues extremely difficult."

You can say that again, Sam.

Poverty, injustice, overbreeding, overpopulation, suffering, oppression, military rule, squalor, torture, terror, massacre: these ancient evils feed and breed on one another in synergistic symbiosis. To break the cycles of pain at least two new forces are required: social equity—and birth control. Population control. Our Hispanic neighbors are groping toward this discovery. If we truly wish to help them we must stop meddling in their domestic troubles and permit them to carry out the social, political, and moral revolution which is both necessary and inevitable.

Or if we must meddle, as we have always done, let us meddle for a change in a constructive way. Stop every *campesino* at our southern border, give him a handgun, a good rifle, and a case of ammunition, and send him home. He will know what to do with our gifts and good wishes. The people know who their enemies are.

Wild Horses

What words, what images, what memories, best evoke the essence of the American West? These are some that come first to mind:

The odor of crushed sage in the hand. The fragrance of burning juniper. A mountain lion crouched on a canyon ledge. The word *canyon* itself. One black vulture soaring in lazy circles above the burning hills and ice-cream-tinted folds of the Painted Desert. Red mountains like mangled iron rising beyond dunes of golden sand. Stone ruins nestled in an alcove of a cliff. The cry of the coyote—first one, then a second, then a chorus as a full moon the color of a blood orange sinks beyond the skyline. The aroma of burning mesquite. One dust devil spinning across an alkali flat. An abandoned Model T Ford sunk fender deep in sand along a back road in the Arizona Strip. The sound, at night, of something bulky and *fierce* crashing through an alder thicket on the slope of Two Medicine Mountain in Glacier National Park—the smell of the grizzly. Red and yellow billboards along old US Highway 66 warning the westbound mo-

torist: 200 MILES OF DESERT AHEAD LAST CHANCE FOR WATER
SEE FREE REPTILE ZOO RICH THICK MALTS GENUINE BEADED
INDIAN MOCCASINS. A real Indian (not merely another "Native
American") riding a genuine pinto horse (not a shiny new pickup
truck). A real old-time ranger with a Smokey Bear hat, mounted
on a big bay, leading a string of pack mules down the switch-
backs of Muley Twist into the wilderness of the Waterpocket
Fold. The smell and creak of saddle leather, the pressure of
stirrups under your boots, the feel of the reins in your hand.
The clank of a turning windmill near an abandoned, broken-
down corral. The smell of horse dung. The smell of horses.
And . . .

Your first sight, at evening, of a file of slick unbranded, un-
claimed, tangle-maned, and broomtailed mustangs coming off
the ridge for water, old mare in the lead, the stallion at the
rear. Wild ones. Wild horses.

The romance of the wild horse haunts the American West
today as much as ever it did in the past. The wild horse is very
much with us, thriving and multiplying in parts of Nevada,
southeastern Oregon, southwestern Wyoming, and the western
deserts of Utah. Protected by Act of Congress since 1971, the
wild mustang has only one common natural enemy: ranchers
and the pet-food industry. Until 1971 most wild horses ended
their careers inside tin cans on supermarket shelves.

Protection of wild horses led to a rapid increase in their
number. Like fruit flies, like humans, like rabbits, the mustang
is a sexy animal, a prolific and fecund beast; given the chance
it multiplies with zest, at an exponential rate. These growing
numbers impose a growing burden on the limited carrying capacity of the range. Wild horses compete not only with cattle
but with other herbivores—deer, elk, bighorn sheep, pronghorn antelope.

Hunters and game-and-fish departments in the Western states

have been slow to perceive that wild horses might eventually threaten the food supply of game animals, as cattle do already. But the moguls of the public-lands beef industry are more alert in protecting their interests. For years cattlemen tolerated a limited number of wild horses because they saw them as a source of income (dog food) and as a replacement pool for draft animals and saddle mounts. But with Congressional protection the wild horses have become numerous enough to affect the ranchers' bank accounts. Highly agitated, vocal, loud, powerful though small in number, the beef ranchers have been demanding that the government reduce and control (at taxpayers' expense) the wild horse herds. At the same time public sentiment—or horse-loving sentimentality—stands firm in defense of the wild horse. Caught between, the bureaucrats of the BLM do their sneaky best, as always, to obey instructions from the beef industry while maintaining a pretense of impartiality. Inevitable conflict: too many people demanding too many things from a finite land and a shrinking resource base. What's the conservationist answer?

The health of the land and the well-being of our native wildlife come first. If as seems obvious the wild horses, like feral burros, are a menace to both land and wildlife, we must then reduce and limit the population of wild horses. I would suggest confining them within a few large desert reserves that are also well-stocked with mountain lions, grizzlies, jaguars, and wolves.

At the same time we should eliminate private cattle from our public lands. Not merely reduce their numbers but remove them entirely. They don't belong there. The public lands should be managed for three purposes only: wildlife habitat, watershed protection, and human adventure—pleasure and recreation.

We don't need range cattle but we do need a few bands of

wild horses here and there, if only to preserve a beautiful tradition. They do belong. They also serve to keep alive some fundamental questions: To whom do the public lands and national forests really belong? For whose benefit should they be managed? And are human needs the only needs worthy of respect?

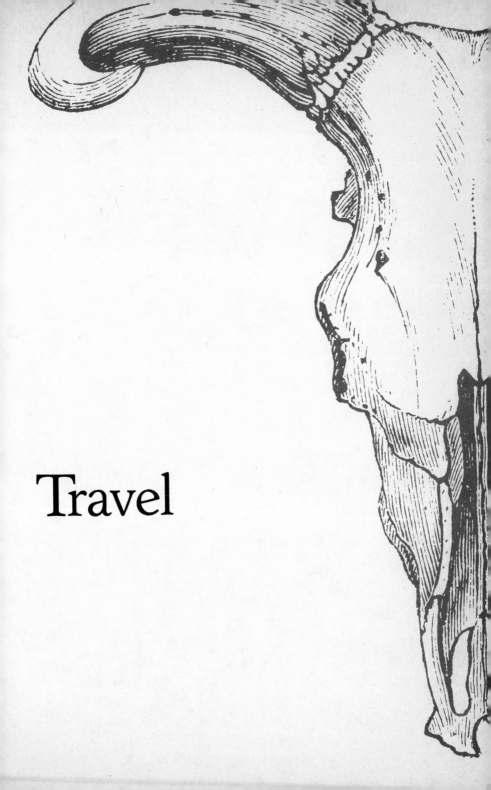

Travel

A San Francisco Journal

Day 1

A child's view of the great world—that's what we're getting today. Flying from Tucson to California, I bring along not only my wife but our three-year-old daughter Rebecca as well. How could we leave young Becky behind? It's her world too and she knows it.

As seems always to happen, we draw seats over the wing. Even so, Becky strains at her seatbelt for a glimpse of the Grand Canyon, of the flat and sunburnt grid of Las Vegas, of Death Valley, and the Sierra Nevada when the pilot announces the approach of each of these wonders. And then we soar above a sea of mashed-potato clouds—nothing below us but billows of foaming vapor—and my kid turns her attention to her coloring book, her snack lunch in its plastic wrap, a stuffed fuzzy toy dog named Snoop.

The clouds scatter as we descend the west side of the mountains. Becky stares down at fields of snow amid dark forests. Well, she has seen that sort of thing before—but not from twenty thousand feet above. We cross the Central Valley, sinking toward Oakland. My kid is fascinated by the glitter of the Bay. All that water. All that glitter. The airfield rises to meet us. Touchdown: the engines roar to break our headlong rush, at three hundred miles per hour, toward another routine flaming airline disaster. Becky cries with delight when she feels the reunion of aircraft and earth. I hope for the best.

The terminal building, in Becky's eyes, becomes another maze of marvels. All those people! Who would believe the world contained so many, such strange busy perfectly fungible multitudes? Like *Crocodile Dundee* in New York (from that dumb but faintly amusing movie) she wants to greet and pass some time with each of the ten thousand abstract strangers rushing toward and past us.

I grab this midget of mine by the arm and hustle her on toward the baggage claim. We ride down an escalator. She loves escalators and wants to do it again. All right, I say, but only one more time, okay? Okay okay, she says. It's much more fun, we agree, to do it backward—up the down and down the up— but the crowds are dense, the security is strict, we dare not mess around. The *San Francisco Examiner* invited me here, at the *Examiner*'s expense, but not to spend a week in jail.

Day 2

The banging and bells of the cable cars wake me up about six in the morning. I look out the window and there is Alcatraz Island again, waiting for me. I'm glad that place has been made into some kind of tourist attraction. All my life I've suffered from the secret dread that I would end up in prison, probably for some crime against the state. But I lead a clean life. I've seen the inside of jail cells only four times so far. (Once was enough.) The charges lacked distinction: vagrancy, reckless driving, public drunkenness, and something the police called "negligent driving," when I overturned my car in a ditch along the interstate highway near Chandler, Arizona.

After breakfast we head downhill for the waterfront, riding the cable car. Becky's idea. She loves it. Better than escalators, better than elevators. We walk the little beach near the Cannery, inspect the retired sailing ship *C. A. Thayer*, the decommissioned ferryboat *Eureka*.

If I were a millionaire—well, a multimillionaire—I'd buy me an old ferryboat like the *Eureka*, make a floating home of it. What a grand ballroom, what a place for parties. And when I tired of the social hubbub, I'd weigh anchor and steam away to some romantic hideaway like Richmond, Oakland, or South San Francisco. East San Mateo too might be worth investigating.

Comparing the crew's quarters with the captain's, in the good ship *Thayer*, I think of Conrad, Jack London, B. Traven. Class distinctions. The social hierarchy. The power of power. The habit of servility. Apologists for the old system tell us that the sailors lived in kennels, the officers in cabins, because the rigors of seafaring life required such radical apartheid. Conrad believed in this convention. Embraced it. Jack London wavered between sympathy for the men and his idolatry of superior force. (Read *The Sea Wolf*.) But Traven—crackpot anarchist, democrat, libertarian—imagined a world, at sea as on land, where all men and women might share in power. (Read *The Death Ship*.) His was the generous vision of human life.

But which vision is the true one? I ask myself. The Vikings cruised the European coasts and crossed the North Atlantic in open ships, each craft with its warrior leader, but all sharing equally in the toil of the voyage and the booty of their conquests. Or take the crude pragmatic view of the matter, as we Americans like to do: What works better—to treat your men like dogs or to deal with them as at least nominal equals? No easy answer to that question either. If power and privilege seem like appealing goals of life, you'd be happier on a nineteenth-century slave ship than on a modern American freighter.

We take a turn around Ghirardelli Square, buy our postcards and our hot dogs on Beach Street, grab the cable car for a ride up the hill. Trying hard to be good tourists.

Day 3

Today I go for a little walk, while my wife and child entertain themselves on the cable cars. I walk down Chestnut Street to the Art Institute and look at the pictures, the sculptures, the posters on the walls, the satisfying variety of traditional bohemian types moving about through the corridors. A good *smell* in the air of old damp stucco, fresh oil paints, hot solder, and hot black coffee. Beards on the boys and hairy legs on the girls— fine artistic nuances everywhere. Was never an artist myself— but I've always envied the artist. So much more dignified and physically pleasing, I like to imagine, to butter a canvas with gory gobs of chrome yellow, or to hack in fury with a rusty hatchet at a redwood log, creating there or thereupon the image, say, of a cow—than to do what I am doing at this moment: pecking daintily with three fingers and a couple of thumbs at this maddening, irritable, neurotic, electric typewriter. The constant humming vibrato is like a toothache on the brain. Yes, I believe in high technology but for Godsake this electrified typing machine—that's a leap too far. Too fast. Too high. Like Herb Caen I am just beginning to get accustomed, after thirty years, to my comfortable, clattering, touch-resistant, Royal manual desk model.

Down to the waterfront again. Like most landlubbers I am fascinated by boats and ships. I pay my two dollars and tour the *Balclutha* (assembled in Glasgow over a century ago) and marvel once again at the complex engineering of an ocean-going sailing ship. The rigging alone is enough to baffle the imagination. But the luxury of the captain's paneled cabin and the bleak dark cramped squalor of the crewmen's hole up forward reminds me of the other ship, the *Thayer*. How could men tolerate such gross inequality? Hard to understand—but they did. For centuries. And in other ways we do the same today.

Past the trawlers and the crab boats, the seafood restaurants and the schlock shops for tourists, I stroll toward the Embarcadero. The trash does not bother me for a moment. Every city has its like. No essential difference, really, between these souvenir stands selling T-shirts and those chic boutiques in Sausalito or Carmel peddling junk that nobody needs to people with more money than anybody needs. At least you can *wear* a T-shirt, soak up some sweat with it while tarring the roof of your penthouse. But what earthly good is an engraved brass gong from Nepal? Maybe you could beat it into a bowl, feed your dog with it. Make a hubcap for your Honda. Hang it from a buckeye tree and catch chestnuts before they bruise themselves on the ground. But what else?

I stop for lunch at a near-empty deli under the shadows of the financial district. The minestrone is cold—I send it back for reheating—but the sourdough bread tastes good as ever. An old acquaintance meets me here. We talk about the film she wants to make, an animal-rights drama based on William Kotzwinkle's *Doctor Rat*. (A good, tough, tear-jerking, little novel, by the way—much more interesting than *E.T.*) She's got a screenplay, a director, a cast; all she needs to complete the package is a minimum of five million dollars.

The towers of high finance loom above our necks. Try pyramid power, I suggest. She smiles, we go our separate ways. I visit the remains, the ruins, of North Beach. The last time I entered this district was in the fall of 1957. When I too was a beatnik. There's not much left that I can recognize or remember except the old City Lights bookshop. Even the honky-tonks are yielding before the relentless expansion of Chinatown. I enter the store, browse on books for a few minutes. It's good to see the complete works of Allen Ginsberg on display. He is not one of my favorite poets. Nevertheless I like to see his little black and white hip-pocket books here. I check a copy of *Howl*: thirty-third printing! Very good.

By the time I get to Market Street (bound for the *Examiner*'s offices) it occurs to me that I need better urban footwear. My feet are jammed, crammed into a pair of Arizona cowboy shoes—pointy toes for kicking snakes, undershot heels for slipping stirrups—and my feet are expanding.

I pause to look about for a decent sort of bootery. Far down Market Street I see the store I want: military surplus. I head in that direction, making my way among the drunks and derelicts, the social castaways on the shore of a desert island made of cement, asphalt, grease, garbage, spittle, iron. Muttered requests for survival reach my ears. I pass out a quarter here, a quarter there, a paper dollar in between. (Spend it wisely, fellows.) Not so much out of Christian charity as from the morbid conviction that I too will more than likely end my days in similar condition.

But not, I pray, on the streets of a roaring city. When my wino days descend upon me I want to enjoy them on the porch of a rotting shack on the bayou or in a crumbling adobe hut under an athel tree beside a spur line of the Southern Pacific Railroad. In the swamps or on the edge of the desert, reading old books, feeding the lizards, awaiting the monthly visit of my personal social welfare lady. (I can see her now: she'll be black, plump, kind, willing to laugh at my ancient bawdy jokes, not too strict about how I spend my relief check.)

I leave the store with my cowboy boots in a plastic bag under my arm and my feet comfortably encased in Vietnam jungle boots from Korea. Size twelve, wide. They cost me twelve dollars each, twenty-four the pair, but I don't mind, nothing is too good for a man's feet if they are good feet. On certain occasions it pays to be extravagant. Humility is a virtue, said Schopenhauer, only in those who have no other.

I make my visit to the newspaper office. I shake hands with young Will Hearst, and with Warren Hinckle, and a number of other good, sound, friendly people. No one says anything about my new shoes. That hurts, a little, but I am presently consoled by the publisher's assistant, Jodi Hoffman, who asks me if I'd like a cash advance against expenses. Could use it, I acknowledge. How much, she asks, $250, $500 . . . ? I shrug as she keeps raising the ante. But life acquires new meaning.

Minutes later I leave the office with this roll in my pocket big enough to choke a cow. One of the editors—David Mc-Cumber—accompanies me to the nearest bar, half a block down the street. We discuss my writing project.

I tell him about my first venture into journalism, during my high-school days back in Stump Creek, Pennsylvania. I took the journalism course in my junior year and flunked it. In my senior year I enrolled in the same course once again; once again I flunked. What was the problem? Never could get the basketball scores right. Spent too much time interviewing the cheerleaders. Wrote too many editorials on death and immortality, forgot all about the junior-senior prom. The journalism teacher urged me to find a more creative field, such as auto mechanics or spot welding.

Getting dark outside. I tramp across Mission and Market and up to the Flag Store at 1047 Polk Street. I know the manager here, Jim Ferrigan. We've done a few boating trips together on the Green and San Juan rivers in southern Utah. Ferrigan is good company on any kind of expedition—a good fireside drinker, a wit, a scholar, a raconteur, a master of the epic shaggy dog story. He is also a master flagman. Ask him any question about flags, about any flag, and nine chances out of ten, impromptu, he'll come up with a complete history not only of the flag in question, its symbolism and heraldry, but of the nation or idea behind the flag.

Take the popular rainbow flag, for example; where did it come from? Designed in 1789 by Thomas Paine, Ferrigan explains, it stands for international peace and brotherhood, for freedom of the high seas and for the rights of man. Among other things. As modified in San Francisco, with a pink stripe sometimes substituted for the infra-red, it symbolizes sexual liberty, i.e., gay rights, free love, lesbian sisterhood, etc. I don't ask Ferrigan what the "etc." represents but I do buy two flags: the traditional Jolly Roger for my riverboat and the rainbow flag (with red stripe) for the flagpole on the roof of our house near Tucson.

Time to head for home. Promised my wife a Hungarian dinner tonight. I march up Polk Street in my creaky new boots, veering off for a side trip over Nob Hill where I pass a couple of grand hotels. I stayed once in the Mark Hopkins, many years ago. When was that? Why? Oh yes—that was the time the *National Geographic* sent me, first class all the way, from my home in Moab, Utah, to Sydney, Australia. They'll never do that again.

Leaving the Top of the Mark behind, probably forever, I bear north-northwest via Taylor and Hyde for my appointed and proper place on Russian Hill.

Day 4

Becky remains enthralled by elevators, escalators, and cable cars. My wife takes her out for more mechanical adventures. I

stand at the picture window of our seventh-floor glassy apartment—mostly windows and mirrored walls—and stare across
the bay at Berkeley, up the bay at Sausalito, downtown toward
the big, hulking, slab-sided skyscrapers of the business district.
I've been asked to attempt comparisons between San Francisco
and other cities of the American West, such as Phoenix, Denver, Salt Lake, Tucson.

I am not well equipped for such a task. I am not a connoisseur
of cities. In general all big cities seem alike to me: appalling
places. Anthills, beehives, termitaria. I generally avoid them.
At present I live within sight of the city of Tucson but do not
expect to stay. The developers have got us surrounded and we
will soon be compelled to flee. Where to next? Our plan calls
for a return to the little town where I lived before—Moab,
Utah, population about five thousand counting dogs and chickens. Tucson was never meant to be more than a temporary
expedient, a return to college for my wife, and in the nine years
we've lived there the population has nearly doubled. Close to
half a million now. That's too many humans in one camp. It's
not sanitary. Not healthy. The air is dirty, the traffic is mur-
derous, the clamor of horns and screams and sirens and crum-
pling metal gets on a man's nerves. They don't even turn off
the lights at night, but despite the glare the crime comes not
in particles but in waves. Steady waves, like the surf at Ocean
Beach. Police helicopters circle the city through the lurid nights.
Our watchdogs, watching us, peering down from time to time
with blue beams of dazzling intensity into backyards, alleyways,
bedroom windows.

Not a wholesome way to live. The Hopi Indians have a word
for it: *koyaanisqatsi*, meaning "life out of balance" or "weird
craziness, man," and the word applies exactly to places like
Tucson, Arizona.

And Tucson remains a small city, though growing like a mel-

anoma on the face of the rare Sonoran desert. Everything unpleasant about Tucson is three times worse in Phoenix, a monster
megalopolis of one and a half million beset, betrayed, belea-
guered souls. Phoenix vies with Denver and Los Angeles for
the filthiest air in the United States. Phoenix should never have
been allowed to happen.

If "progress" means change for the better—and I'll support
that—then Growth as we have come to know it means change
for the worse. Let me try out another new-fangled maxim here:
Growth is the enemy of progress.

Look around you and see what Growth has done to your city.
"A city not growing is dying," says Dianne Feinstein, mayor of
San Francisco. Really? You sure?

Why not consider the possibility that a city, like a man or
woman or tree or any other healthy living thing, should grow
until it reaches maturity—and then stop? Who wants to live
forever under the stress, strain, and awkwardness of adolescence? Life begins at maturity. A human who never stopped
growing would be a freak, a mutant, a monster, a sideshow
geek eating live chickens for supper and toppling dead of dia-
betes and kidney failure into an early grave. We passed the
optimum point of urban growth and population increase many
decades ago. Now we live in the age of accelerating growth and
diminishing returns.

Think of it this way, Mayor Feinstein: When a city finally
stops growing its citizens can finally begin to live. In peace.
Security. With a modicum of domestic tranquillity.

Day 5

We borrow a fat Ford from the newspaper motor pool and
plunge south along Highway 1, bound for Pacifica, El Granada,
Half Moon Bay, Pescadero, and Santa Cruz.

The great green waves of the Pacific come crashing in, each

crest unfurling in a flag of foam. The surfers are at play, paddling seaward to meet their appointed swell, standing then to ride it to the beach, bright boards skimming across the rising wall of water. A daring and dashing sport, a game—it seems to me—for heroes.

I romanticize. Think of the music of the Beach Boys: jolly music, crude, frisky. Not exactly heroic. Carefree is the word.

We enter Half Moon Bay, where I lived in the winter of 1957–58. Smell of rotting brussels sprouts. Field on field of artichokes. The long gray beach trampled by a million feet, littered as usual with filter tips and wadded Kleenex. What was I doing in Half Moon Bay?

Speak, memory!

I was a member of Wallace Stegner's creative writing workshop at Stanford. Two days a week I cranked up my 1952 Chevrolet pickup—rust-red with rotted floorboards; you could see the asphalt rushing below between your feet—and commuted over the pine and eucalyptus hills to Palo Alto. I was at work on a sensational new kind of American novel that winter. The subject was sub-bohemian life and the desperate search by young Americans for spiritual enlightenment, emotional fulfillment, sexual liberation, escape from the chores of the workplace and the routines of domestic bondage. My characters spent a great part of their days and nights smoking giant joints, drinking red wine by the jugful (Gallo's Hearty Burgundy), and racing back and forth across the continent from Green Witch Village, New York, to North Beach, California, in borrowed, stolen, unpaid-for, and boat-shaped automobiles. My title for the book was *Down the Road*. I never finished it, for reasons now historical which I have successfully blotted from my mind.

But I remember our days in Half Moon Bay. I was married then, as I often have been. My wife painted pictures—pictures of the inner life—on huge canvases hard to get through the front door. Our two-year-old son toddled about among the hydrangeas in the backyard digging live snails out of their shells with his little finger and eating them. *Escargots vivants*, snot-green, squirming, juicy snails. I sat in a tiny room off the kitchen with my typewriter propped catty-cornered on a shelf to avoid the steady drip of rainwater from the leak in the ceiling. I too had to sit in a hunched and skewed position, as I typed, to keep the water off my left shoulder. We complained to the landlord about the leaks in early October, when the first steady Pacific drizzles arrived. Sometime in late March, when the rains slack-ened, the landlord had the roof repaired.

Meantime we watched the banana slugs crawl up the win-dowpanes leaving their trails of slime across the glass, listened to the boom of the sea on the waterfront, and went for long walks in the evenings through the fog and mist, crunching unavoidable snails underfoot at every step, yearning like home-sick children for the sun and heat and harsh dry air of the desert. In early April I gave up the fellowship of Stanford's creative writers to take a job as a firefighter in the Gila National Forest of New Mexico. I didn't really want to be a writer anyhow. The work was too confining. Let Kerouac do it, if he still wants to. (Whatever became of that fellow anyhow? Seems like so many have come, have flourished, have faded and disappeared, and here I am still typing, still tramping on.)

Onward.

The highway rises above the coastline south of Half Moon Bay. We pause at overlook points to stare at the sea below, beating itself to a milky froth against the black rocks at the base of the cliff. WARNING! says a signboard: HIKING AND CLIMBING PROHIBITED IN THIS AREA.

The road seems crowded with too many cars. A steady stream of sleek metallic mollusks, each with pale pink fleshy organisms crouched inside, pours along Highway 1 in opposite directions. What are all these idiots doing out here, I snarl in exasperation;

why don't they stay home where they belong? Easy, dear, easy, says my wife; it's a holiday weekend. So it is. We're headed for Santa Cruz to share a Thanksgiving dinner with my sister and her family.

But holiday or not, my overwhelming impression of San Francisco, of the Bay Area, of northern California in general, is one of congestion. Of overwhelming congestion. Of a rapidly approaching terminal compaction. The steel gridlock that will finalize the end of the open road.

We stop at the beach at Pescadero for a close look at the surging ocean. My barefoot daughter dances along the edge of the advancing and withdrawing tongues of foam. She laughs with delight, running over the firm wet sand, escaping then caught by the forward slide of the water. Everything that happens is a joy to her—or a momentary tragedy. Watching a happy child at play—and for a happy child life is nothing but play—the observer could easily persuade himself that life is nothing but a prolonged bumpy decline from the high point of birth. We start at the top and work our way downhill, making a hard complicated job of it, until we reach the bottom of existence in the arms of mortuary science. A sick sad defeatist thought that I entertain only in my weakest moments. Only a fool envies the joy of a child; a grown-up man or woman shares in that joy.

We pass pigpens, sheepfolds, cow pastures, and old gray farmhouses set within windbreaks of pine and eucalyptus trees. Heartening to see a few farms still surviving along this western coast, among the outliers of the growing, advancing, ever-expanding, always-growing, urban complex (perplex?) behind yonder eastern hills. This shoreline has not been fully developed yet; may it never be.

More acres of artichokes appear, with here and there a green field radiant with a rash, a bonfire, of bright glowing orange pumpkins. I think of pie. I think of marinated hearts. Bless the land, from which all blessings flow.

Christmas-tree plantations. More groves of leprous-looking eucalyptus, that Australian immigrant. Not a bad tree. In fact a handsome tree. Makes good firewood. Graces the air with a sweet nutty fragrance when it burns. I smell it now.

We pause on another high vista for another view of the grand Pacific. Breakers crash against the headlands north and south; towering billows of water thunder against the battered granite a hundred feet below. I think of Tennyson's eagle:

> *The wrinkled sea beneath him crawls; . . .*
> *He watches from his mountain walls,*
> *And like a thunderbolt he falls.*

And of Elinor Wylie:

> *Avoid the polluted herd,*
> *Shun the reeking flock;*
> *Live like that stoic bird*
> *The eagle on the rock.*

Poets. Misanthropes. We must be approaching Robinson Jeffers territory:

> *I'd sooner, except the penalties,*
> *kill a man than a hawk.*

Yes, he wrote that line, that Jeffers. Shocking sentiment.

Day 6

Leaving wife and child at my sister's place near Santa Cruz, I drive south along the coast alone, bound for Monterey, Carmel, the Big Sur. Last time I drove this road was in the spring of 1958. Things have changed a bit, somewhat, in the usual way. That is, more of the same and much more of it. Santa Cruz is a lovely town—but there's too much. Monterey and Carmel are beautiful as ever—but in excess. Again, as everywhere in California, the principal effect is one of glut—too many. Too much of everything. Too many boutiques in the shopping malls. Too many shopping malls. Too many cars on the highway. Too many highways—the road map of Northern California looks like a web of varicosis. Necrotic varicosis. Too many rich fat expensive houses crowding the shores and hillsides. Too many towns. Glut and gluttony—a paradox—too much of both.

You had a good thing here in California but you overdid it.

We had a good thing in America but got carried away. The carefree exuberance of a wildly successful nation, dedicated to the youthful proposition that too much is not enough, is destroying the basis of our wealth and happiness.

I'm circling cautiously around the touchy subject that my whining inevitably leads to: too many people. Industrial development and urban expansion encourage population growth. Population growth encourages industrial development and urban expansion. Each tendency reinforces the other. We have trapped ourselves in a vicious circle, a viscous cycle, of mutually destructive Growth models.

I can see only two possible solutions: reduce our material standard of living to something like the Asiatic level, thus providing the room and the means for further population growth; or keep our techno-toys, our cars, our boats, our ample suburbs, our shopping centers, and consumption malls, but restrict further population growth, put a brake on the breeding spree with a view to eventually reducing the American population (by normal attrition) to a sane, rational, manageable number. About one hundred million? Fifty million? Ten million? The optimum figure can be determined later; what matters here is the principle: no more growth. Social progress, yes; bulk Growth, no.

(Imagine a Northern California where one-half of the human population suddenly, magically, painlessly disappears. Vanishes, like a bad dream. Imagine the results. Rents go down. The price of a house or condo drops through the floor. The cost of land goes down. Small farms and ranches again become available to the poor but enterprising. Food, clothing, wheels, gadgets, go down in price. But at the same time there is an increased demand for labor, skilled and unskilled, in essential industries, such as the production of food and fiber: wages go up. And everywhere, in the towns, cities, and countryside, open space appears: the streets and roads are no longer jammed, the parks and forests and beaches no longer crowded. The decibel level goes down by half. The air becomes clear and clean again. Mountain streams, perhaps after a time even some rivers, become pure enough to drink from. As they were before and as they were always meant to be. The conventional grow-or-die economists would dispute this vision of a possible future but then they are the most fanatical ideologists of our time; furthermore they are always wrong. Economics is not only the "dismal science," as Malthus called it; it is also the most dismally obtuse of the sciences. Economics, no matter how econometric it pretends to be, resembles meteorology more than mathematics. A cloudy science of swirling vapors, signifying nothing.)

How to reduce the human population of Santa Cruz, of California, of America? Without undue pain to anyone but land speculators, development planners, the sharks and barracudas of real estate? My answer is simple: Place a good stiff tax on Motherhood. Penalize parents. Revise the tax system so as to reward singles and childless couples while requiring the begetters of children (including me) to pay more, not less, in taxes.

Economic incentives, if properly designed, should do the trick, thus achieving the end desired without curtailing personal liberties. What could be more fair, in a society like ours, where all goods and bads are measured in dollars?

So far so good, a few may agree, but what about the poor, the under- and nonemployed who are, as social classes go, the most profligate producers of children? (The word *proletarian*, you may recall, means reproducer, those whose only service to the state consists in the production of children.) Here, too, my device of economic rewards and penalties can be applied. Why not, for example, offer a brand-new Mustang convertible to every girl who consents to having her fallopian tubes tied in a Gordian knot? This would be much cheaper, in both the short and long run, than continuing the present system of welfare payments to those millions of teenagers and young women who have reached the conclusion that being welfare mothers is the only career open to them. It would have the additional benefit of eliminating from the gene pool those stupid enough to consent to such a deal.

And males, you ask, what about them? Well, since one male can easily pollinate a hundred females a year (and be glad to have the work) sterilizing boys and men would not be cost-effective.

I am well aware that such modest proposals might be greeted in some circles with shocked incredulity. Racism! they'll cry. Genocide! Eugenics! Bad manners! And so forth.

Not true. My program of painless population reduction applies to every sector of the American anthill. All are eligible to participate; no one is excluded.

Most people are not qualified to have children anyway. Look at them. Look at yourselves. Look at me. How many of us can honestly say that we have the skill, the intuition, the understanding, the economic means, to be really good parents? Of all our many freedoms in America, the right to breed is the one most grossly abused. Parenthood must be redefined—in our overcrowded world—as a privilege, not a right. As a reward, not a duty. The license to reproduce oneself, in cooperation with that special other, should be earned, not given. We must learn to think not only logically but biologically.

Then there's the delicate question of immigration, legal and illegal, and its effect upon the dream of the good life in our America.

The good life. In our America. That is really what I've been thinking about all along as me and my Ford creep forward, from red light to red light, through the opulent edge of Monterey, of Carmel.

Steinbeck country? Robinson Jeffers country? No, this is Clint Eastwood country. Ronald Reagan country. And why not? Hollywood has created and defined our basic dreams for more than half a century; why not let movie actors take over public administration? America and Hollywood: they deserve each other.

As for immigration, I'll get into that tomorrow. Maybe. Scratching my shanks—one of the pleasures of poison oak—I drive on toward Big Sur. God bless America, let's save some of it.

Day 7

Late afternoon. Alarmed by the density of the traffic on this coastal highway, I hurry on past Point Lobos toward the strung-out community of Big Sur, hoping to find lodging there for the night. A foolish hope. Since I've failed, as usual, to make reservations, I find no room available. Nothing but NO VACANCY signs everywhere I turn.

Darkness is coming on and I don't have even a sleeping bag with me. I turn and join the northbound stream of traffic crawling back toward Carmel. The traffic condenses. I find a turnout not fully occupied, park the car, and go down over the bluff for a walk on the beach.

The western horizon is an indefinable meld of sky, cloud, and sea, with one glimmering blood-red track leading straight to the dying light. Tide coming in: the waves surge upon the beach, shatter themselves against the rocks. I feel a resonating vibration in the hard wet sand beneath my feet. Nobody walks this strand but myself, sandpipers, a few screaming gulls. And maybe the ghost of Robinson Jeffers:

> *Gray steel, cloud-shadow-stained,*
> *The ocean takes the last lights of evening.*
> *Loud is the voice and the foam lead-color,*
> *And flood-tide devours the sands . . .*

I climb the winding path up the hill, through mats of ice plant, a scrubby growth of manzanita, the familiar skein of paper tissues, old sun-bleached Fritos bags, the traditional bouquets of toilet paper. Those trivial but tender tokens of our intimacy with nature. Without a bit of trash here and there would Nature even look natural anymore? One American philosopher—I think it was Mencken—defined the out-of-doors as a good place to throw beercans on a Sunday afternoon.

Locked into a steel chain of auto traffic probably ten miles long, I creep on wheels—stop, advance ten feet, stop again, advance again—toward Monterey, City of a Thousand Motels.

All full. I am tempted to commit an act of vagrancy, make a public nuisance of myself by discharging a pint of rented beer into the gutters of this clean, honest, reputable town, thus gaining free lodging for the night in the city jail.

Instead I spend the night in a Motel 6 off 101 in Salinas. Don't get many opportunities to enjoy expense-account living, might as well make the most of it before these decent Hearst people realize what a fraud they have—if only temporarily—employed. I lull myself to sleep with cable TV, searching up and down through ninety-nine channels for something fit for a family man to watch. I keep hearing about too much sex and female nudity on television; where is it? I am forced to settle for an ancient Cary Grant film run through a vat of living color, where all the actors including Grant appear to be suffering from what our folks back in Appalachia call the "yeller janders."

Day 8

In the morning, following Mimi Sheraton's advice, I take my breakfast at the nearest Winchell's Donut House. I am surrounded by field hands from a Viva Zapata movie, all wearing crumpled straw hats, K-Mart windbreakers, and speaking only Mexican. A ring of tired, solemn, weatherbeaten, brown faces with drooping mustaches. Big hands with grimy fingernails.

Since I seem to have made overpopulation a theme of this journal perhaps I should touch now upon the touchy subject of immigration. I am against it, whether legal or illegal, whether from Latin America or from any other source. Yes, I acknowledge that we are all the descendants of illegal aliens—including the American Indians, who apparently crossed the Bering Strait or land bridge only twenty thousand years ago. But sooner or later we must draw the line, say No More, our boat is full. Enough is enough. We are not morally obliged, for example, to serve as Mexico's "safety valve." Let us seal the border now, militarize it if necessary, and force the government of Mexico (if there is one) to face up to the nut of the problem created by a population that keeps doubling every thirty years. Mexico needs not more loans—money that will end up in the Swiss bank accounts of *los ricos*—but a revolution. A complete revolution, not communist, not capitalist, but moral: a revolt against injustice, cruelty, oppression, squalor and—most obvious—a woman's rebellion against Our Lady of Perpetual Pregnancy.

Oh yes, I grant you, we need such a revolution back in Appalachia too. And in Newark, N.J. And in my adopted home of Moab, Utah.

(How many children have you begat, Abbey? I've fathered four. But I've been married five times. That comes to only 0.8 child per marriage. If every American couple would exercise similar restraint, we'd make a better, roomier, healthier America within two generations. Remember: *Growth is the enemy of progress.*)

Backtracking to Carmel, Boutique City by the Bay, where the population's chief industry appears to be—shopping. Parking and shopping. The teenager's notion of Paradise. No doubt there are worse ways to live out one's existence. Pecking away all day at computer keyboards in Connecticut, perhaps. Supervising motor traffic in New York's Holland Tunnel. Crawling on bloody and gangrenous stumps down the sidewalks of Calcutta, city of joy, during evening rush hour, with Mother Teresa whispering in your ear, "Lighten up, boy, lighten up."

Clogged arteries of asphalt. Occluded intestines of cement. Wedging my Ford into a mass of parking-lot metal steaming under the sun, I make my way on foot to Tor House and Hawk Tower, the former home of Robinson Jeffers. This is a literary pilgrimage to the shrine of one of America's best, most reclusive, least known and most unpopular poets.

I walk down a street shaded by eucalyptus, Aleppo pine, and Monterey cypress, past million-dollar houses with four-car garages to find Jeffers's place exactly where he built it seventy years ago, the stone house, the stone tower, both looking strangely small, quaint, almost Disneyesque under the looming walls of the adjacent mansions. Jeffers and his wife, Una, came here in

1917 to escape the pressures of urban life. ("Tor" means something like a high, lonesome, craggy hill.) The hill remains, and not far below, the sea still bashes itself against the granite of which Jeffers's house was made, but the poet's once-isolated home has long since been surrounded and nearly digested by Our Lady of Perpetual Growth. Jeffers, the poet of seascape and rock, of hawks and shepherds and the bleak freedom of solitude, lived long enough (until 1962) to see his refuge become no more than high-bracket real estate. There is more than irony here; there is absurdity. The poet himself was not surprised; like Cassandra, an accurate prophet, he anticipated the whole business:

> *The extraordinary patience of things!*
> *This beautiful place defaced with a crop of suburban*
> *   houses—*
> *How beautiful when we first beheld it.*
> *Unbroken field of poppy and lupine walled with clean*
> *   cliffs,*
> *No intrusion but two or three horses pasturing . . .*
> *Now the spoiler has come; does it [the place] care?*
> *Not faintly. It has all time. It knows the people are a*
> *   tide*
> *That swells and in time will ebb, and all*
> *Their works dissolve . . .*

Like others, I admire Jeffers but do not love him. He was not a wholly lovable man; not in his poetry: too grim, humorless, genuinely misanthropic, his entrails consumed by some secret bitterness. He told the truth in his work and nothing but the truth (a rare thing in poetry) but did not tell the whole truth. He could see joy in the lives of sea gulls and falcons, horses, hummingbirds, and dolphins, but not in the games and comedies of his fellow humans. There is grandeur in his verse, as in the roll of the sea against the Carmel rocks, but the music is a melancholy, dirgelike monotone.

After an hour of brooding on Hawk Tower, I feel the need for a different kind of outlook. I buckle myself into my motorcar and bear south again for the Big Sur coast. For Partington Ridge. For the spirit of Henry Miller.

Day 9

Armed with a stiff loaf of sourdough bread, a pound of Danish cheese, and a bottle of California red, I work my way carefully down a steep and sandy trail to a cove in the cliffs. There's a lovely beach down there, apparently deserted despite the endless currents of auto traffic on the highway. Time for a private picnic in the sun, while the combers charge like cavalry, foaming and braying, against this splendid, shining, rock-girded coast.

Drove all the way to San Simeon last night for shelter and am retracing the route, returning to The City. Doing my vacation the hard, rigorous way, the American way, motorized and merciless. Dodging the road kill and tailgating those traffic-obstructing fools in front of me. Now I need an hour of rest.

I reach the bottom of the long descent. Almost. About twenty feet of near-vertical alluvium separates me from the bright sand, the ebbing surf. I peer cautiously over the brink, searching for the route down. Under the bluff, enjoying themselves in the sunshine but concealed from the highway above, are two men with their pants off, committing a deviant act. I withdraw quietly, not disturbing them, and clamber up the long steep tricky path to my car. Well—I don't care what consenting adults do to each other in the privacy of their bedrooms. But why on a public beach? They might frighten the sea lions. They certainly spoiled my lunch.

Driving on under the tawny golden mountains, above the cliffs and the wrinkled Pacific, I come to a sign that says ESALEN INSTITUTE, BY RESERVATION ONLY. I've heard of this place. Curious, I turn down the paved driveway into a grove of trees, a scatter of redwood cabins, masses of parked automobiles of mostly Nipponese extraction. Among the trees I can see clusters of people sitting in circles, stroking one another with benign smiles and sympathetic, understanding eyes.

I come to another sign: STOP, PLEASE. I stop. A young bearded man in chinos, polo shirt, and sandals steps out of a sort of guard shack or sentry box. He confronts me with tender eyes, a warm rich benevolent smile, a moment of brotherly love.

My type don't belong here and I know it. Guilty as sin, I mumble, "Just looking around."

Still beaming, he says, "We appreciate your interest but we're having a closed seminar now. Would you mind coming some other time? Please?"

I've always been a sucker for the Christian cold shoulder. Meekly I turn my car around.

"Have a nice day," he says, waving good-bye.

Don't tell me what kind of day to have, I'm thinking. I'll have whatever kind of day I want. But I leave quietly.

Early in the afternoon I take a room at the Big Sur Inn. My room, a small one, for singles only, is called the Petite Cuisine. Cute as a periwinkle. The room directly across the hall is the Honeymoon. Through its closed door I hear girlish giggles, the creak of bedsprings. Ah, young love! Smiling, I pull on my new walking shoes and go for a hike up Castro Canyon. My objective is the top of the mountain, the old coast road, a glimpse of the Ventana wilderness to the east.

The trail follows a little stream, winding around the roots of mighty redwoods. Clear water tinkles over rock. The trail forks and forks again, petering out less than half a mile from the Inn. I scramble up the south side of the canyon, through sword fern, laurel, and second-growth redwoods, until I arrive at the spine of an open ridge leading toward the summit still a couple of thousand feet above.

There's an old sheep fence here. On the other side of the fence is what looks like an abandoned jeep trail. I step across the fence and take the jeep trail up the mountain. A steep grade but easy walking. Now far below is Highway 1, the endless traffic, the glittering sea. The hills are covered with tawny grass; in the hollows grow the rugged, handsome California oaks. A few beef cows range a distant fenceline. One vulture patrols the air. Crisscrossing vapor trails unravel and dissolve against the blue, far above. I sit down on a high point to peel an orange.

Hearing voices, I look up to see a party of hikers descending the trail road toward me. In the lead is a tall, thin, young man who looks exactly like what's-his-name, the lead singer of that band called Fleetwood Mac. But my true love, Stevie Nix— Nixie?—Nicks?—is not with him. So to hell with him. He stops beside me.

"Hello," he says, "where you from?"

"Arizona," I say, "how about you?"

"We live here," he says. "This is our ranch." A significant pause. "You're trespassing."

"Just following this old road," I explain.

"You must have crossed a fence somewhere."

"I didn't see any fence." I point down into Castro Canyon. "I came up the side of the hill."

That mollifies him somewhat. "Okay," he says, "as long as you're here you might as well enjoy it. But don't build any fires. And don't stay up here after sundown, you'll get lost for sure. Nobody would ever find you."

I promise to do as instructed. He and his little group go on down the hill. I wait until they are out of sight, then continue up the hill, into the evening. Four deer watch me from a nearby hillside. A doe crosses the trail above, sees me, and stops. She looks back at something following and in a moment her fawn appears. They both stare at me. I step forward, they bound away.

An hour later, near sundown, I reach the top of the main ridge. The jeep trail ends at the side of a passable graded dirt road. On my right is a steel gate shut and locked with six—not one, but six—heavy-duty padlocks. The fence bristles with Keep Out signs. One of them goes into detail:

ALL PERSONS FOUND PICNICKING, CAMPING, BUILDING FIRES, MUTILATING TREES OR SHRUBS, REMOVING ROCKS, SOIL OR OTHER MATERIALS, DUMPING RUBBISH, FISHING, HUNTING, SHOOTING, OR TRESPASSING WILL BE PROSECUTED.

Beyond and below, to the east, lies a deep and wooded valley, and a branch of the Big Sur river, with higher, stonier, meaner-looking mountains beyond. La Ventana wilderness. Some distance to the north stands Pico Blanco, one of the more prominent and famous peaks of the coastal range. The officials of a mining company propose to stripmine limestone there.

John Steinbeck describes this area in a fine short story called "Flight."

The stillness up here, some 2,800 feet above the shore, seems absolute at the moment. I can hear nothing but the singing of the blood in my ears. Nor see any sign of man or woman but this private road, that padlocked gate.

Why so many locks? Why such a vehement warning sign? I

feel sympathy for any landowner feeling so besieged and threatened by tourists like me. But I also feel sympathy for the landless, the uprooted, the disinherited, for all the poor city mobs who have no home to call their own but a few cells in the urban and suburban hive. What kind of citizenship is that? Whatever became of Jefferson's dream of a nation of independent freeholders? What happens to democracy when 2 percent of America's families—according to Federal Reserve Board reports—control 40 percent of our national wealth? When 10 percent control 80 percent? We're drifting toward an El Salvadoran, Latin American form of income redistribution. Lincoln defined democracy as government not only for and of the people but *by* the people. Sounds like a good idea. We should try it sometime in America.

The sun blinks out below the far edge of the Pacific. The air becomes chilly with premonition. I turn and descend the way I've come, a mite hastily, following the old trail-road down through the lavender twilight, through a chorus of dying crickets, under emerging constellations, into the pitch dark of the redwood forest deep in Castro Canyon. But I keep to the road, crossing not a single fence, and find my way easily back to Deetjen's Big Sur Inn in time for dinner at the family table.

I'll have the leg of lamb, please. With a glass or two of claret wine on the side. And yes, I'll take a second helping of your soup.

When I return to my room, La Petite Cuisine, I see the Honeymooners reentering theirs: two neat trim clean-cut young men, holding hands.

Day 10

I pause for a few minutes at the Henry Miller Memorial Library, a private institution open to the public, for a few words with an old friend of Miller's, the artist Emil White. He autographs a book and a poster for me. "Yes," says Mr. White, a little shaky at eighty-five but his mind still clear, "Henry and I were good friends. But Henry had many good friends. Everyone who knew him loved him."

Miller dedicated his book *Big Sur and the Oranges of Hieronymus Bosch* to Emil White. Near the end of this casual collection of sketches and memories (published in 1957) he writes:

> . . . I sometimes think how wonderful will be the day when all these mountainsides are filled with habitations, when the slopes are terraced with fields, when flowers burst forth everywhere. . . . I try to imagine what it may be like a hundred, five hundred years hence. I picture villas dotting the slopes, and colossal stairways curving down to the sea where boats lie at anchor, their colorful sails unfurled. . . . I see ledges cut into the cliffs, to give purchase to chapels and monasteries suspended between heaven and earth, as in Greece. I see tables spread under brilliant awnings (as in the time of the Doges), and wine flowing into golden goblets, and over the glitter of gold and purple I hear laughter, laughter like purling rapids rising from thousands of jubilant throats. . . . Yes, I can visualize multitudes living where now there are only a few scattered families. There is room here for thousands upon thousands to come . . .

Old Henry had a generous spirit. Seeing the Big Sur as a potential American Sorrento or Amalfi, he was eager to share it. Quite the opposite to Robinson Jeffers. The only paradise, thought Miller, is that which all can share. A true and lovable sentiment. But—how many is that "all"? Carmel, Monterey, Santa Cruz, San Jose, San Mateo, were once each a bit of paradise too. The truth must lie in the tension between the bitter realism of Jeffers and Miller's sweet idealism.

Back to San Francisco via Santa Cruz and Highway 17. Over the hills to the bay again, trapped in a millrace of streaming traffic, threatened fore and aft and on either side by rumbling eighteen-wheelers, I make a momentary mistake and find myself, five minutes later, lost in the true horror of Santa Clara and San Jose. It takes me thirty minutes to grope my way back to the freeway again. *Koyaanisqatsi!* How can humans endure this mad mechanical circus? No one should have to live this way.

Onward, onward, past Stanford and Redwood City, San Mateo and South San Francisco. Into The City, through the park, into the tunnel under the Presidio and there it is, the Golden Gate. I turn right at the right moment and am rewarded with the view of Alcatraz.

Home again.

Day 11

Reunited with my little family, we cross the bridge into Marin County, check out Muir Woods, Stinson Beach, Bolinas, watch the sun set one more time over the far Pacific Ocean. Already homesick for the Southwest, we eat our supper at Juan's Mexican restaurant in Sausalito. Tomorrow my wife and child fly back to Tucson.

Days 12, 13, 14

Alone in this glossy, glassy, postmodernist unisex apartment with only an electro-throbbing IBM Selectric III for companionship, I stare out the windows, drink much coffee, type too many words. A cruel hard way to make a living: some day I hope to give up typing forever, for as long as the rivers flow, the grass shall grow, and switch to an honest trade—shoe repair, perhaps; game poaching; cattle stealing; white slavery; and gun running.

I am relieved from my journalistic duties by a phone call from another old friend in this city, Kevin Briggs, a "head-hunter" by profession (manager of an employment agency). To-morrow is Sunday, he says, December the seventh; let's get bombed. Let's remember Pearl Harbor as we did the Alamo!

With Ferrigan the Master Flagman we meet at a bar on Lombard Street called Shea's. WE CHEAT DRUNKS AND TOUR-ISTS, says the printed awning over the entrance. From there we go to Edinburgh Castle, where I get sentimental at the sound of bagpipes. Then up Polk Street to another bar, the name of which has vanished from my memory. The only "straight" bar on Polk, says Ferrigan. The place is quiet, uncrowded. The Polkettes—teenage punkers from everywhere—slither past on the street outside. We climb Nob Hill to the Fairmont, where we duck into the gentlemen's room for urgent relief. Then down the hill into Chinatown and the bar named after Li Po, another favorite poet. Behind the bar smiles the Eurasian bartender Nancy, one of the world's most beautiful women. For the third or fourth time this evening I fall in love.

After some time at Li Po's we proceed to a Basque restaurant in North Beach for a dinner of soup, fish, salad, beefsteak, and dark red wine in an unlabeled bottle. I don't know what Mimi Sheraton would think but it tastes mighty good to me. I'm satisfied now, ready to go home, but Ferrigan and Briggs insist on one more bar for the ritual nightcap. We step out into the street again, past the strip joints; the barkers try to lure us in. "We live here," snarls Ferrigan, his feelings wounded. "One of us must look like a tourist," Briggs suggests.

Into another nameless bar, where I am served something

hot, smooth, sweet, insidious. The decibel level is deafening; a roar of chatter comes from every side, violent music rises from the floor, from the walls, but all about me are the most distinguished-looking women I have ever seen—tall, blond, Nordic, elegantly dressed—not pretty but *handsome*—engaged in drowned, mute, but brilliant conversations. Perhaps it's all a mime, a dumbshow. Whatever the case, I am struck once again by the painful realization that there are worlds out there I shall never know, pleasures and refinements I could never understand. Not in Moab, Utah; not in Oracle, Arizona; not in a hundred years.

I guess I'll have to live with that. My friends see me home by taxi.

Day 15

The morning is clear but windy: whitecaps on the Bay. By noon the wind has died, the waves relax, the weekend fleets of sailboats venture out. From my window they appear, at first glance, like a hundred varicolored butterflies, wings erect, drifting on the water.

Briggs and Ferrigan arrive to take me for a boat ride out of Sausalito. We head for the Golden Gate, pausing briefly at the old gun emplacements below the Presidio: Ferrigan the historian explains the tactics of coastal defense, the difference between direct fire and plunging fire, the fine art of trajectory. Briggs points out the poison oak which I wish I had noticed two weeks ago.

We drive onto the bridge, passing the antisuicide railing at the near end, and the low easy rail beyond. My friends explain: the barricade rail prevents the distraught from leaping onto the roof of the historic brick fortress below, where Park Service guides lead daily tours. That's the rule of the bridge. You may, if you insist, jump into the water; you may not bombard our rooftops with falling bodies. Fair enough.

We park in a muddy lot by the Sausalito docks. A fantastic array of anarchical houseboats crowds the water; it looks like a scene from Hong Kong. Children, birds, dogs, cats run up and down the floating walkways, walled on each side by this delightful variety of idiosyncratic boats and houseboats, some riding high, a few listing badly, but each one different, all looking lived-in, worn, frayed, comfortable as old shoes. Curtains and potted plants adorn every window, the one common feature.

I follow Ferrigan and Briggs over the walkways, which tend to sink beneath our weight, here and there, to shoe-top level. Smell of woodsmoke on the air, the aroma of burning hemp; this is not Fisherman's Wharf. We are greeted by friendly faces despite the notice near the entrance: THIS AREA UNSAFE FOR TOURISTS. Briggs is known here.

Left, right, straight ahead, the path leads in various directions. I'd never find my way out of here in the dark. Finally we enter one of the houseboats, I am introduced to our hosts, Steve and Pam, and a cluster of children. Also present, having arrived before us, is Briggs's woman-friend Margaret. After a deal of talk, beer drinking, and casual preparations, we are led onto Steve's boat, a thirty-foot, all-wooden, lap-straked, sailing sloop. The boat has an antique, handmade, informal look about it, cluttered with loose gear and empty beercans, and needs a new paint job. But it floats, it functions, the auxiliary inboard engine putters below, under the cabin floor. There is no wheel; this boat is steered the old-fashioned way, with a hand tiller mounted directly to the rudder. Guiding the tiller with one foot, Steve backs the boat slowly from the dock and into open water. We turn, sails furled, and motor off into Richardson Bay, bearing more or less for Tiburon and Angel Island.

Ferrigan runs two flags up the halyards: one blue and white

with the words DON'T GIVE UP THE SHIP stitched across the middle, the other black with white skeleton holding an hour-glass—the personal flag of Edward Teach, pirate. The hourglass on the flag symbolizes time, of course, but more explicitly Your Time—Your Time Has Come. Edward Teach led a jolly life as a pirate but lasted only two years.

Steve cuts the motor, unfurls the sails fore and aft. We drift for a while with the breeze and the outgoing tide. A cooler is broached, the Steam beer broken out; a platter of fried chicken, prepared by Briggs himself, magically appears. Eating, drinking, talking of sand sharks and abalone, great white sharks and Belvedere real estate, we sail past a houseboat disguised as a tiny isle with palm trees, then into Raccoon Strait. Steve fires up the motor again and steers us into the yacht basin of Tiburon. Our primitive craft from the hippie slums of Sausalito glides into dock among sleek hydrofoils, catamarans, snow-white sailboats, and immaculate cabin cruisers of one-hundred-percent virgin fiberglass. The yachtspeople of Tiburon, lounging on the open deck of Sam's Bar, glance our way now and then, too polite to stare.

What are people like us doing in a place like this? I whisper to Briggs.

Attracting attention, he says.

We pass an hour at the dockside bar, renting the beer, eating the chips and guacamole dip, eyeing the young barmaids in their miniskirts, listening to Ferrigan discourse on the history of Alcatraz and Steve describe how his boat was built, Tom Sawyer fashion, with volunteer labor, improvised skills, materials scavenged from the garbage dump, and no blueprints.

The sun sinks low. In misty twilight we return to our boat, cast off, motor out into the strait and around the point, and cruise back across the shining waters, through the rip tide, toward the soft lights of Sausalito. Sitting on the plywood roof of the cabin, I look forward at the proud Homeric curving prow, the air-piercing bowsprit and taut jibsail. Yes, I think, this must be the way. For one day at least I've forgotten the deserts of Arizona, the red-rock canyons of Utah, the erosion of the West, the politics of national redemption. To hell with all that.

Good-bye, San Francisco. Queen of American cities, fare thee well.

Lake Powell
by Houseboat

Who could resist the invitation to spend a week on a fifty-two-foot houseboat on Lake Powell (Jewel of the Colorado River) amid the scenic grandeur of southern Utah's wild red-rock canyon country? Free?

Well, I could.

I could resist it. I did have better things to do that week. Like installing a new wood-burning stove in our living room, a chore that included connecting a six-inch stovepipe to a seven-inch chimney flue. Or finishing my study of Gibbon's *Decline and Fall*, a literary task I'd assigned myself thirty-two years ago and still not completed. Or sitting down at the typewriter to face once again the awful, blank, impassable abyss of page one, chapter one, part one, of one more final great American novel.

But then I thought of that juniper tree. I mean the juniper tree that grows from a crack in the rock on the rim of a place called the Rincon, one thousand feet above what was the river and is now Lake Powell. I thought of that lone juniper, the hard turquoise-blue berries shining on the dark green of its foliage, the cedarlike incense of its red-lined bark, the twisted form of its trunk and the cockeyed upreach of its limbs, the look of things that live for five hundred years—and go on living. The ongoing, ever-growing ceremony of life.

The lake itself, I'll confess, also provoked a certain morbid curiosity. A part of my heart lies buried beneath that enormous pond; it was time to see once again, after an absence of many years, the shimmer of brassy waters under the sun, the tapestried walls of half-sunken canyons, the crooked little grottoes that wind back into the underworld of stone. If they were still there. A man's first love is the most intense. Whatever the case, I'm a desert dweller and desert dwellers love water. Lake Powell, though a recent and artificial creation, is the largest body of water in the American Southwest.

I accepted the invitation. We met in early October at a place called Hall's Crossing in Utah, a small marina near the middle of the eastern shore of Lake Powell. My hosts were a group of geologists from Dartmouth College, among them Professors Robert Reynolds and Charles Drake and recent graduates Billy Condit, Randy Spydell, Dave Merritt, and Hendrik van Oss, together with about thirty students. This was to be a field trip made on water.

I hadn't met any of these people before, but as I walked down the floating steel dock toward a cluster of giant metallic houseboats resembling water-borne Winnebagos, I felt that I was probably in the correct neighborhood. And when a young man approached wearing khaki shirt and pants and on his head a cap that said ROX, I knew I was among the right party. This was Hendrik van Oss, and as he shook my right hand he pressed a bottle of Molson ale into my left. I was introduced to the professors and assigned a bunk in one of the three rented houseboats. When, late in the afternoon, the last of the students finally arrived, we slipped moorings and chugged majestically out of the marina toward our first campsite on the far shore of

Lake Powell, away from the all-night lights and all-night roar of Hall's Crossing's diesel generators.

A sallow desert sun floated beyond an overcast sky. A cold breeze stirred ripples on the flat surface of the water. One large bird, maybe a great blue heron, maybe a wood ibis, soared in lazy circles—nothing better to do—above the pink and rosy domes of sandstone that wall in this portion of the lake. The students, a lively mixture of sophomores and juniors of both sexes, swarmed over the houseboats in search of living space, ignoring the splendor of the scenery. And why not? We'd be surrounded by nothing but splendid scenery for the next seven days. The moment the boats were tied up on the west shore and the motors shut off, half of them stripped down to swimsuits and plunged into the fifty-four-degree water. The sight chilled my thin, lukewarm Southern blood; I was happy to join the executive session in the master salon of the cook boat, where the professors and other aristocracy of the expedition had gathered about a table laden with Scotch, gin, vodka, sound bourbon whiskey, and various edibles—baby clams, fried oysters, cheese, crackers, stuffed and pickled jalapeño peppers. There can be nothing jollier than geologists on a field survey, especially when far from home.

After dinner the students built a bonfire of driftwood on the dried muck and gravel of the shore. There are few sand beaches along the margins of Lake Powell. Under the bright stars and new moon, the collegiate singing began. I contributed the first line of the only Ivy League song that occurred to me: "Far above Cayuga's waters . . ."

And the chorus promptly answered: ". . . There's an awful smell . . ."

Up with the dawn, for the days were getting shorter, we steered the three houseboats north-northeast toward the upper end of the lake, a professor or instructor at the helm of each. These

boats sleep twelve to fourteen and move at an optimum cruis-
ing speed of five miles an hour, powered by twin 75-horsepower
Johnson outboards that consume one gallon of fuel per mile.
Since Lake Powell is often swept by sudden winds and lash-
ing storms, with few shelters, it is a dangerous place for small
craft. Unless you can afford to rent or buy a houseboat or cabin
cruiser, such as you see at the marinas of Lake Powell, this lake
is not for me or you. Powell is a playpen for the wealthy.

Lake Powell is not, properly speaking, a lake anyway. It is
a man-made impoundment created by the completion of Glen
Canyon Dam in 1962, a 180-mile-long water-storage reservoir.
Submerged three hundred to four hundred feet beneath the
surface lies the old channel of the Colorado River and most of
the original Glen Canyon, a once lovely wonderland of grottoes,
alcoves, Indian ruins, natural stone arches, cottonwood groves,
springs and seeps and hanging gardens of ivy, columbine, and
maidenhair fern—and many other rare things. These were delights formerly enjoyed, easily and cheaply, by thousands of
Boy Scouts, Campfire Girls, and others floating down the lei-
surely river in anything they wished—rowboats, canoes, kayaks, rubber rafts, old inner tubes.

Because it is not a natural lake, the shoreline of Lake Powell
is constantly rising or falling, advancing or receding according
to the power and water demands regulated by the outflow through
Glen Canyon Dam. As a result, Lake Powell's canyon walls are
coated with what is known as the Bathtub Ring, a grayish-white
horizontal band of silt, salts, and minerals. Where the shoreline
is open, broken by bays or side canyons, you will find an extensive area of drying mud and mud-covered trees and shrub-
bery—all dead. This Dead Zone, as some call it, may extend
for miles into lateral areas, depending on the volume of the
most recent drawdown of water. A ten-foot vertical drawdown,
for example, can expose a hundred square miles of barren waste

where nothing survives but tamarisk and tumbleweed. And flies. And maggots.

As we advanced up the windy lake toward Castle Butte, our destination for the night, the professors paused from time to time to give lectures and to discuss the names and nature of the stratified rock formations rising on either side of the lake. Red rock, gray rock, buff, amber, yellow rock—Kayenta, Chinle, Wingate, Navajo, Carmel, Entrada, the names have a fine and ancient ring about them. Millions of years in geo-logic were batted around like shuttlecocks as we sailed into the dip of the land, into older layers of the earth's crust, further and further into what geologists call deep time. *Deep time*—another noble phrase.

I was pleased to learn that although the surface of the lake seems motionless, stagnant as a swamp pond, the current of the ancient Colorado River continues to flow hundreds of feet below, a ghost river still bound, as it has been for eons and epochs, toward the Sea of Cortez and the Pacific Ocean. I was even more pleased to learn that sedimentation is proceeding rapidly and that the useful life of the reservoir and dam is probably limited to no more than three hundred years. By A.D. 2283, Lake Powell will have become a delta of mud overgrown with tamarisk jungles, and the dam itself, its penstocks blocked, will be transformed into a splendid waterfall. Good news!

Meanwhile, little fleets of grebes dodged our approach, ducking under the water like mechanical toys. Unidentified ducks winged off into the distance in V-formation. We saw few other signs of life except the scattered craft of die-hard sport fishermen. Lake Powell is much beloved by anglers, its waters teeming with rock bass, striped bass, bluegill, channel catfish, sunfish, and even rainbow trout. The lake is contaminated by various metals from upstream mills, however, so that there is a continuing controversy over the health risks in eating the fish. I asked geobiologist Randy Spydell if he'd be willing to eat fish caught in Lake Powell. No thanks, he said.

We tied up the boats in a cove under the shadow of Castle Butte, a thousand-foot monument of sandstone. I walked along the Dead Zone, through the usual litter of a popular Lake Powell campsite: beercans, bait cans, old tennis shoes, dirty underwear, fire rings heaped with mud, charred sticks, tinfoil, and onion skins. Although the lake has eighteen hundred miles of shoreline, most is steep or vertical stone, leaving about 5 percent that is suitable for camping; these areas receive heavy usage during the busy summer months. Trashy places, I reflected, tend to attract (present company excepted) trashy people. And what can be trashier than rich white trash? But the sun was still shining; I went for a swim and a bath in the cool green water, floating on my back among clots of algae. It looked like algae; I hoped it was algae.

That night I lay on my bedroll on the flat roof of Professor Reynolds's houseboat and watched glittering Orion blaze overhead and green-gold meteors slash across the sky. Despite the garbage, I thought, and despite the damnation of the dam, this is still a magnificent place to be. And to be in. Far up Red Canyon on our right, where a stony ravine and the red cliffs and an old-time prospectors' jeep trail led deep into the wilderness, I heard a great horned owl calling somebody's name.

The next night we camped near the head of the lake at the mouth of Dark Canyon, a well-named place walled in by sinister, overwhelming cliffs that rise fifteen hundred feet above the water. The wind blew, clouds arrived, the dark sky rained on us all night long. We cowered in our bunks and listened to the sound of ancient Permian cannonballs, untouched by any human hand or agency, tumbling down from terrace to terrace and crashing like bombs into the lake.

No visit to the canyon country is complete without a storm. The next day was bright, clear, glorious with blue sky and golden sunshine. Ephemeral waterfalls poured from high ledges. We motored down the lake, past the confluence with the Dirty Devil River, past North Wash, Trachyte Canyon, Ticaboo Canyon, Sundog Bar, Good Hope Bar, Tapestry Wall, Blue Notch Canyon and the Horn, and Castle Butte once more, where petrified logs lie decaying—eon by eon—in the open air. We looked for bighorn sheep and bald eagles along the canyon rims and stopped again in the middle of the lake for a swim. Mossback and Shinarump formations revealed themselves on far-off stratified walls. Above the walls we saw the domes, fins, pinnacles, and surreal hills, like melted elephants, of the Navajo sandstone, miles and miles of a fantasy landscape stretching away toward the ten-thousand- and eleven-thousand-foot peaks of the remote Henry Mountains. The mountains were covered with snow that had fallen the night before. "Wouldn't want to be up there now," an old cowboy once said to me, "with only my spurs on." True fact, Slim.

As we lay on the roof of our houseboat that night, camped in the outlet of Seven Mile Canyon, the students and I heard a yipping, barking noise from up on the mesa wastelands. "What was that?" somebody asked.

I thought. "The *vox*," I said.

"A fox?"

"The *vox clamantis in deserto.*" A cry of Dartmouth in the wild.

The next day we sailed to the south and west under gorgeous red skies at dawn. Sailors take warning. A chill wind raised whitecaps on the lake, but the mixture of sunlight and cloud shadow created lovely, photogenic effects on the world of nude stone that embraces the reservoir. Early in the afternoon we anchored the houseboats ashore at the Rincon, where an abandoned meander of the old Colorado River had carved a horseshoe-shaped canyon a thousand feet deep. While the geologists went about their field studies, I hiked up another trail road that leads out of the Rincon by way of a fault line on the east wall. The old road is an eroded ruin now; no jeep, wagon, or power-wagon has passed this way for many years. As I climbed through the fault in the Wingate and entered the dark red Kayenta and then the buff-colored Navajo, I left behind the Triassic Age and walked into the Jurassic, me and the flying reptiles.

I reached high ground up among the great sandstone hummocks hundreds of feet high that occupy thousands of square miles along the Colorado River. There I saw potholes full of the recent rainwater, bayonetlike yuccas, dark green junipers growing from clefts in the rock, and in the sculptured grooves of little gorges the bright green-gold shivering leaves of cottonwood trees. There was coyote scat on the old trail and the heart-shaped imprint of mule deer in the red sand. I felt better when I saw that. It eased the guilt of houseboat travel.

I paused for a look around the horizon. From where I stood the paved highway to Hall's Crossing was thirty to forty miles away by land. Between lay a canyon-carved territory inhabited only by deer, coyote, and feral crossbred cattle. Far out there, as I remembered, like a mirage in the dunes, was a World War II half-track personnel carrier half-buried in sand, and a sun-bleached notice at the turnoff from the highway that said: WARNING: 4-WHEEL DRIVE ONLY. CARRY PLENTY OF GAS & WATER. VISITORS ARE ADVISED TO REGISTER WITH SHERIFF'S OFFICE BEFORE ENTERING THIS REGION.

A cheery, heartwarming sign. It's good to know that places remain in the Lower Forty-eight where a man can get into deep trouble all by himself, without any help from others.

I climbed to the summit of the sandstone domes. From there I could see Navajo Mountain to the south, the fifty-mile-long

Kaiparowits Plateau on the west, the Henrys to the northwest, and various named and nameless buttes and mesas standing to the north and northeast. One thing more: on the next promontory of rock, overlooking the Rincon and the inner canyon, I saw a lone juniper tree lifting shaggy arms toward the blue sky. I remembered that tree. After twenty-five years of war and terror, elections and assassinations, triumph and calamity, my juniper stood firmly in place, a trifle older but otherwise unchanged, still alive, rooted in stone. This, too, was good to know. Though much has been lost, much remains.

The sun had gone down. The brief desert twilight was yielding rapidly to night. I was astonished to discover that I had walked for at least five miles in my happy, solitary, melancholy reverie. It was high time to return to the merry geologists, the warmth of new friends, and the smell of a good Dartmouth field dinner. There would be music, another student bonfire on the rocks, and afterward the womblike comfort of my mummy bag on the rooftop dormitory, under the world's sharpest, keenest, friendliest display of stars. There is much to be said for our American way of anarchy, after all. As civilizations come and go, rise, decline, and fall, ours is a pretty damn good one. Most things considered. While it lasts.

By the light of the fresh and fattening moon I walked homeward to the boats.

River Solitaire

A Daybook

At Saturday noon, on November third, a few days before the last general election, I rowed a small skiff into the current of the Colorado River, near the town of Moab, Utah, and disappeared for ten days.

By choice. Since I lacked the power to make a somewhat disagreeable world of public events disappear, I chose to disappear from that world myself. This was easily arranged. Nobody goes down the river—not the turbid, muddy, freezing snowmelt of the Colorado—in November. I was assured of having the river to myself. I preferred this kind of solitude not out of selfishness but out of generosity; in my sullen mood I was doing my fellow humans (such as they are) a favor by going away.

A friend from Moab saw me off. Another friend—Ken Sanders—would meet me at the end of my solo journey, seventy miles downstream at a nowhere place known as Spanish Bottom. From there we planned to run the rest of the river together, my little rowboat following his big pontoon raft through Cataract

Canyon, rejoining American culture (such as it is) at the Hite
Marina on Lake Powell.

In my boat I carried enough food for two weeks, a one-man
tent, a sleeping bag, some warm clothes in a rubberized bag,
five gallons of drinking water, and the many other little items
needed for a week or more in the wilds—cigars, bourbon, the
Portable Tolstoy, matches, Demerol tablets, pen, notebook, a
.357 and a P-38.

We launched ourselves, my little boat and I, onto the flowing
river. Here is what happened:

Saturday

We float beneath the bridge. From the shade I gain a splendid
view of the Moab valley, a vale of greenery walled in by red
sandstone cliffs. Beyond the cliffs rise the snow-crowned La Sal
Mountains, only fifteen miles away by line of sight. Valley, cliffs,
mountains—one of the world's most magnificent settings for a
human community. Unfortunately the town of Moab (about five
thousand people) was overrun by the uranium industry back in
the 1950s and remains an eyesore, a commercial-industrial slum.
But that junk will rot and fade from the scene, given time, as
a thousand other ephemerid boomtowns have vanished from
the landscape of the American West, leaving what *belongs* here:
some farms, a few little ranches, the original Moab, the national
parks, and perhaps, someday, a small college and arts center.

I row past the uranium mill, which is at present shut down,
silent, empty except for a cadre of supervisors, watchmen,
maintenance men. Like most people in the Moab area, I hope
it stays this way—silent. But the enormous twenty-acre slime
pit of uranium wastes remains in place beside the mill, on the
shore of the river, a constant threat to the health and well-
being of every living thing downwind and downstream.

The river flows around a swampy bottomland and enters the Portal—a fifteen-hundred-foot-deep notch in the red-rock wall, the gateway to what, only three decades ago, was still terra incognita: the canyonlands, the Needles, the Maze, the Confluence, Monument Basin, the grabens, the Fins, the Henry Mountains, the deep, intricate, uninhabited marvels of the Glen and Escalante Canyons. Half of this grandeur now lies submerged (for the time being) under the stagnant waters of artificial Lake Powell. But much remains. More than enough to make a journey into this region, whether by foot or horse or boat, still a delight for anyone who loves the primitive, the deep time of ancient stone, the bedrock foundation of soil, grass, flesh, spirit, life.

A few great blue herons stalk the sandbars, and many ducks—pintail, mallard, cinnamon teal—drift on the water. The mudslides of beaver indent the banks. A few hawks soar overhead. In the jungles of tamarisk and willow on the riverbank I can hear the quiet chirping—not often—of little birds. Black-throated sparrows? Towhees? Verdins? Not many around, this time of year, and the few that stay through autumn and winter are quiet birds.

I pass a trailerhouse and mine workings on the left bank; then a potash mill on the right bank, an enormous silent exotic structure of grotesque design, poisonous green in color, where a dozen men are employed in the monitoring of machines that pump liquefied potash from three thousand feet below. A few cars stand parked inside the high-security fence; a wisp of steam rises from a pipe; the hum of electrical motors seeps through the metal walls; but human beings themselves are nowhere in sight. The plant is like an installation from Mars or Saturn—vast, complicated, sinister, an alien presence. I row vigorously for a few minutes until the bend of the river takes me beyond sight and sound of the mill. Again I am surrounded by desert, by red-rock walls and towering cliffs, and feel as if I have escaped the surveillance of hostile and otherworldly eyes.

Sun going down behind the western rim. I row and float another mile, another, looking through the chilling twilight for a place to camp. The river is walled by mudbanks and jungles of tamarisk on either side, permitting no place to land. I am cold, tired, hungry, anxious to get out of my little rowboat before darkness sets in.

A ledge of rock slopes up from the water on the right. I bear for that, tether my skiff to a willow tree, and make camp for the night. The sky is clear, the stars bright and steady. I do not bother to pitch the tent. I build a fire of twigs and grill two pork chops over the flames. A beautiful night, beginning early. I drink a cup of cocoa and slip into my old greasy sleeping bag, using a lifejacket for a pillow. I fall asleep to the sound of water gurgling past the ledge, the whisper of a breeze through the dry dead leaves of the willow.

Sunday

The November nights are long. I wake in the dark, check my antique pocketwatch by flashlight: five o'clock. I rise and build another little fire on the coals of the one before, make myself a mug of tea. Tea, an apple, a slice of bread with jam, is all the breakfast I require. I load my gear into the boat, untie the bowline, climb aboard, and shove off into the current. Starlight glitters on the silent river, flowing smooth and heavy as oil toward the west. I stroke the water with my oars, guiding the boat onto the bubble line of foam that indicates the center of the current, then ship oars and let the boat turn idly on the stream, floating without effort through the morning stillness.

The east glows with color. The highest canyon walls, two thousand feet above the river, take on the radiance of dawn.

The river flows in absolute silence between mudbanks crowded with more willow, tamarisk, and cottonwood. A mute but bitter struggle goes on there—the invading, exotic tamarisk striving to drive out the native willow.

Deer tracks on the mud and sandbars. Signs of raccoon, beaver, fox, and coyote. And again the birds—heron, sandpiper, killdeer, chukar.

Late in the morning the sun clears the vertical walls, shining down on me and skiff and water and the narrow strip of plant life on either bank. At noon I pull to shore and walk for a mile up sandstone ledges into a cul-de-sac, the closed end of a box canyon. I eat my lunch of raisins and cheese beside a pool of liquid quicksand under a two-hundred-foot overhanging pour-off—a dry waterfall.

Back to the river, drawn by the powerful tug of the stream. I see a bunch of deer, five does, passing like shadows through the trees and brush on the left bank. Two of them emerge from the jungle and step out on a sandbar for a drink from the river. Oars at rest, I glide past within twenty feet of their alert eyes and ears. They see me as only another piece of floating driftwood. If I had my bow now, and one broadhead arrow, I'd be feasting on poached liver and short ribs for supper. Maybe.

I make camp at mile twenty-five, on a sand island in the middle of the river. A fine campsite, at first glance: clean brown sand, plenty of driftwood for a fire, a splendid view upriver of the red-rock cliffs, the golden clouds.

Three o'clock in the afternoon. With the sun going down by five, I am determined to cook my supper by daylight. There is nothing more unsatisfactory than cooking and eating in the dark. I explore the island, gather wood, build a fire on the damp sand near my boat, and fix a supper of chicken and rice, with a miniature bottle of rum and one fat cigar from Safeway (Garcia y Vega) for dessert.

The sun goes down, the temperature drops ten, twenty, thirty degrees—within thirty minutes. Cold on this slender isle, the icy Rocky Mountain waters rolling by on either side. The sky is clear, clusters of stars like blazing chandeliers hanging overhead. A chill wind blows in from the north. I pitch the little tent—may need all the insulation I can get tonight. I put on thermal underwear, crawl into my mummy bag, and read Tolstoy by candlelight for as long as I can stay awake. "The hero of my tale," he writes, "is truth." How true.

The wind moans about the tentflaps. I blow out the candle around eight o'clock and pull the hood of the bag above my ears. A long and bitterly cold night—should have known better than to camp on a sandbar. I do know better—but did it anyhow. Who can resist the appeal of a little, lonesome, one-man island in the middle of a great river?

Monday

In the morning I find my tent stiff with frost. Ice tinkles in the water jug when I raise it to my lips. I build a twig fire in the twilight of dawn and boil a pot of water for coffee.

Two ravens flap across the river, silent, bound in a straight line toward business of importance. A V-formation of ducks flutters by overhead, headed downriver. As I load and launch my rowboat I hear the splash of beaver sliding down their mudbanks into the water. I pull into the stream through the shade of the cliffs, under an overcast sky. My breath vaporizes when I exhale. The one thing we do not need, I think, wishing I had the power not even to mention it in my mind, is a storm. I don't mind being cold; I can bear getting wet; but I loathe the two together.

Don't think about it. Keep going. Once we get to Spanish Bottom we'll set up camp in some rocky nook with a southern exposure and let the wind rave, the sleet come down, the snow blanket everything. If I'd been ready, I recall, I could have taken that deer: I've got the Ruger .357 Magnum in the big ammo can, bedded between two loaves of bread. Loaded? Oh yes.

Eleven A.M. Weather improving, at the moment. I drift downstream on water like oily glass, aided by a gentle breeze that blows, for once, not against but with the current. The sunshine is pallid but warm, the sun barely visible behind the scrim of haze. We are headed due south into the sun.

The river is low. I go with the current, seeking the deepest channel, following the line of foam, the outside of the bends, under the overhanging walls, where the current of the river goes. Watch for mud, sandbars, waterlogged snags: I'd hate to have to get out into this forty-degree water to drag the boat free from some obstacle.

I pass more side canyons—Lathrop, Buck, others without names. Should stop and explore but the mouths of each are choked with a slough of quicksand, a jungle of brush. You'd have to fight your way in there with a machete or else slog through muck up to your thighs. Or both.

The willows, mountain ash, and cottonwoods wear their autumn colors—bright gold against the somber red of the Moen-kopi mudstones, the dark brown Cutler sandstone. The tamarisk is a rusty orange. Stands of wild cane with snowy seed plumes lean with the breeze, then snap back to an upright stance.

There's a giant cottonwood log balanced on a rock, twenty feet above the present waterline, revealing an old high-water mark. Beyond the living things at the river's edge rise the walls of rock, nude red sculptured stone surmounted by gargoyles, beaked heads, godlike profiles from the ancient times. Now and then I catch a glimpse of the high plateaus beyond the middle ground: the high rimrock of Dead Horse Point, Hatch Point,

Needles Overlook, Grandview Point, Island in the Sky, Junction Butte. Most of these are places inaccessible from the river, cut off by perpendicular walls, one above another, of rotten rock.

I tie up my boat at the mouth of Indian Creek, on the left, and follow a deer path along the ledges into the canyon. I inspect the small Anasazi ruins in a cave—mounds of dust, stone parapets mortared with mud, the smoke-blackened ceiling, the potsherds and tiny corncobs, the usual clots of bat guano back in the corners—and then go on, through the clean clear light, up the canyon along a trickling stream. I pass more golden cottonwoods, each one special, unique, like humans, each displaying its individuality with a distinctive *flourish* of limbs, branches, masses of gold and green-gold leaves. The tracks and droppings of bighorn sheep precede me on the trail.

The canyon boxes up; I come to a vertical slot in the stone through which a cascade of silvery water pours, crashing down on the terraces below. The soothing white noise of falling water fills the canyon. Here I pause for an hour of abundant nothingness.

Returning to my boat, I become aware of the silence closing in again. As always when I'm alone in a deep and solitary canyon, I become intensely aware of the stillness around me, of a need to be strictly attentive, fully alert, cautious, and delicate with every step, as if I were under some kind of preternatural observation. *Something is watching you*, I think—though I don't for a moment allow the notion to take full possession of my mind. The feeling has nothing to do with fear; there is no fear in it but simply the belief, the intuition, the conviction, that I should proceed as quietly and respectfully as possible.

Back on the river and down to the mouth of Monument Creek. I explore this canyon too but don't get far: one mile from the river I come to another box, another overhanging spout with classic dripping spring far above my head. Returning to the river by a different route I jump a bunch of mule deer from their shady place underneath the alders. I hear a loud *thump!* as they go bounding—not running—toward the shore.

Early in the evening I select my third campsite, a clean open bench of stone on the left bank, eleven miles upstream from the confluence of the Colorado and Green Rivers.

Beef stew for supper. A near full moon rises through a notch in the walls around me, barely visible through a dense overcast. No stars in sight. The air is cold and still, feeling like rain, or maybe snow. I set up the tent, then go for a walk along an old trail switchbacking up a talus slope. Topping out on a saddle of level stone, I find myself looking down on the Colorado River flowing in opposite directions—westward on one hand, northeast on the other. I am standing on the neck of a big meander called the Loop.

I hear no sound but the coursing of the blood through my ears. A world of stillness without even the whisper of a wind. Nothing in motion but the gleaming river four hundred feet below, the faint advance of moonlight across dark battlements of stone. Stealthily, afraid to attract attention by making noise, I pick my way back down the trail to camp. The moon, encircled by a rust-colored corona, grows dimmer by the minute behind the cloud cover.

Tuesday

Up at six. The dense cloud cover remains but there is not a breath of wind. Tea, bread, and jam for breakfast. I load my boat and push onto the river an hour later. Fifteen miles to Spanish Bottom, foot trails to the outer world, and our rendezvous point. The threat of bad weather now seems trivial; I am delighted with this solitary journey and regret only that it seems to be going so fast. Too fast.

Solitary: but not lonely. I've been too busy to be lonely. Navigating the river, trying to avoid gravel bars, hiking side canyons, hunting for a campsite, making camp, reading Tolstoy—I've hardly had a chance to even feel alone. Floating and contemplating keeps me busy.

Well, enough dawdling, row this boat. Best to set up base camp before the storm actually arrives and the rains come down. Followed by hail. Topped off by snow. Going around the Loop, I row four miles to arrive at a point about a quarter mile from where I started. But that's the way the canyons go, serpentine. Except for crystals and stratigraphy, there are few straight lines in nature.

Strange birdcries in the distance. A heron honking? Coyote scat and deer sign in every canyon. Beaver slides on the mudbanks. Quiet little anonymous birds flitting about in the brush. And autumn color everywhere: bright orange of alder, gold of cottonwood, red of ivy and scrub oak, copper of willows, tawny brown of grasses and greasewood, pale yellow of mountain mahogany, the dark olive green of junipers and piñon pine on the rim above, and along the water's edge the tamarisk thickets, red as rust.

I keep hoping for a glimpse of bighorn sheep—no show. But there's one little brown cricket in the boat with me, chirping now and then. Last of a dying breed this time of year. I'm glad the cricket's aboard: means good luck. Everybody knows that.

Close to noon the sky clears a bit and I catch a look at the sun drifting across a tiny patch of blue. We make a halt below the mouth of Salt Creek Canyon, tie up to a willow and climb out on a limestone ledge. Groping for a better hold I see a cluster of fossil crinoids beneath my hand: the span of ages between my fingertips.

I walk for several miles up Salt Creek, following the clear stream as it pours through slick grooves and chutes in the polished limestone of the creekbed. My boots clash through layers of fallen gold leaves when I pass beneath the cottonwood trees. I climb around a fifty-foot waterfall, scrambling up from ledge to ledge, and walk for another mile before my way is blocked by a high dropoff that I lack either motivation or skill to climb.

By midafternoon, in my boat again, I approach the confluence of the two great desert rivers. As always, I feel a strange excitement in my heart. I row through a blast of headwinds coming upstream, work around a final bend, and there it is—greenish Colorado merging with the golden-hued Green. My friend Sanders will be coming down that latter river. Just for the hell of it, I row up the Green River as far as I can, hugging the bank, and slipping from eddy to eddy. Half a mile and I give it up, ferry across the stream and drift downriver with the main current.

The wind grows rapidly stronger. Three miles to Spanish Bottom. I row against the wind, against the alarming waves topped with whitecaps, and have to strain at the oars before I finally reach the little silty beach at the upper end of the Bottom. I make camp at evening among the boulders, fix my supper of beef soup and crackers washed down with spring water and a slug of Jim Beam's Choice.

Clouding up again. Reluctantly, but glad I've brought it, I erect the old Springbar tent in a grove of sheltering hackberry trees above the beach, then go for a walk through intermittent moonlight across the broad fields, half a mile wide and close to a mile long, of Spanish Bottom. Cottonwoods shiver in the wind and a herd of mule deer—I count seventeen—bound across my path, fifty yards ahead. Canyon walls a thousand feet high rise on all sides but there is one trail up out of here, leading to a maze of pinnacles known as the Doll's House, and beyond that to the Maze, Lizard Rock, the Golden Stairs, Flint Trail, and the high plateau country of Land's End.

At the southern corner of Spanish Bottom I hear the roar of the first big rapid, the entrance to Cataract Canyon. STOP, says a signboard on the right bank, facing the river; HAZARDOUS RAPIDS 200 YARDS AHEAD. Quite so; that's the way we'll go when Sanders gets here, down the river through twenty miles of white water until we reach the stagnant waters of Lake Powell and the end of our journey.

I gaze for a long while on the turbulent waves of the rapid, silvery and phosphorescent in the moonlight, before returning to camp, my tent, the welcome warmth of my sleeping bag.

Wednesday, Thursday, Friday

For three days I wait. I spend one whole day in the tent, reading, while icy rain pours down outside, then the next two days climbing the trail to the hoodoo land of rock above, exploring a number of coves and grottos and box canyons between the Doll's House and the Confluence Overlook, descending at night. I find a new arch, unmarked on the topographic maps and unknown to the Park Service (as I later learned). I name it Deception Arch, its archness not apparent until you get within fifty yards of it.

Sanders is supposed to be here Thursday. Returning to camp by flashlight and moonlight, Thursday night, I am disappointed to discover that he has not arrived. For the first time in my solitary week on the river I feel a twinge of true loneliness, melancholy triggered by failed expectation.

A final day of explorations. High on the sandstone benches above the river I find a series of potholes full of rain water. The water is cold but not nearly so cold as the river. I fill my canteens then take a soapless bath, scrubbing myself with fine sand, drying my body in the wind and the glare of the sunlight. Cold, fierce, exhilarating sensations. Thirty, forty miles away, across the red wilderness of canyons and spires and needles and buttes, the thirteen-thousand-foot peaks of the La Sal Mountains gleam with power, covered with fresh snow.

Much later, after dark, I stand at the top of the trail and look down on Spanish Bottom, fifteen hundred feet below. I see no flicker of campfire at our appointed meeting place. Disappointed again, doubly disappointed, I pick my way down the rocky trail by flashlight and trudge across the long weedy flats to camp, hearing the sound of the wind in the trees, the distant surflike mutter of the rapids at the mouth of Cataract Canyon. I foresee another night with only Leo Tolstoy for company. Tolstoy is good company but he's dead; there comes a time when you long for something more—vivacious.

I enter the grove of hackberrys where I've pitched my tent. I hear voices and see, now and at last, the glow of a fire. Below, under the sandbanks, out of sight from above, stands Ken Sanders with his arm around his girlfriend Lynn, three T-bone steaks grilling on the flames, and a case of Dos Equis waiting at their feet.

Glory be.

River of
No Return

*E*verybody has to go down
the river sometime. What river? Well, *some* river. Some kind
of river. Huck Finn said that, and if he didn't he should have
said it. If he didn't I will.

My sense of obligation, I guess, is the main reason I find
myself, one bright clear morning in July, about to launch forth
on the wavy green waters of Idaho's Salmon River. I have run
a few other rivers, rowed, paddled, drifted down most of the
Green, the Colorado, the Rio Grande, the San Juan—all in the
American Southwest—and even two rivers in Alaska, the Tat-
shenshini and the Kongakut. But never yet been on or even
near the Salmon, one of the most famous of them all. I am
obliged, therefore, to be here, morally required, you might say,
to crawl onto that boat—a rubber raft in this case—and watch
the oarsman point its nose downstream.

I am not alone, being one among twenty passengers plus a
crew of four professional boatmen and river guides. Our out-
fitter is called Echo, a California company based in Oakland,

which operates river trips all over the American West. The four crewmen are John Storrer of Santa Barbara; Dave Burke from Modesto, California; Jeff Wysong from "no place in paticular" but mostly Oregon; and Cort Conley of Cambridge, Idaho. The passengers come from many places—from New York City, from Chicago, from California, from Colorado, and Arizona. They range in age from twelve to sixty-five, in river-running experience from many trips on many rivers to none. It doesn't matter; before this voyage is done we will become, as I have witnessed on every river journey yet, one anarchic but reasonably happy family. It seldom fails: there's something about a progress down a river that brings out the best in anyone. Getting bored with your neuroses? Drop your analyst—drop him/her like a cold potato—and make tracks for the nearest river.

"If there is magic on this planet," wrote Loren Eiseley, somewhere (I quote from memory), "it lies in flowing water." Amen.

The loading of the four seventeen-foot inflatable rafts—made of a nylon-Hypalon fabric—takes no more than an hour, a fairly simple matter of piling on and roping down the waterproof dunnage bags. But the four boatmen had been here hours earlier, pumping the rafts full of air, stowing aboard the many items of equipment needed on a six-day, ninety-mile float trip: cooking gear, water jugs, ice chests packed with perishables, tents, first-aid kit, war surplus ammo cans loaded with bread, crackers, cookies, canned goods, condiments, pastas, repair kits, and spare oars and extra lines and, as usual on a river expedition, an enormous amount of canned beer.

One of the four rafts is a paddle boat, meaning that it will carry no cargo but people, four to eight of them, each armed with a canoe paddle to propel the vessel downstream and through the rapids that lie ahead. The boatmen call for volunteers and six of us step into the paddle boat; one of the boatmen—Jeff—takes a place on the stern of the craft to act as captain. "Forward!" he commands, and we dip paddles into the clear cool water and lurch into the current. Two boats are already on the river and ahead of us; the fourth lags behind.

Down the river we go, with the steep slopes of the canyon, covered with a dense growth of lodgepole and Ponderosa pine, of quaking aspen and Douglas fir, rising high on either side. The course of the Salmon River is called a canyon but resembles a deep, narrow mountain valley. The highest parts of this "canyon" stand six thousand feet above but cannot be seen from the river. Beyond the remote and forested ridges are the rugged mountain ranges of north-central Idaho: the Sawtooth, the Bitterroot, the Yellowjacket, the Clearwater, the Lemhi, Lost River, and White Cloud Mountains. Romantic names, but the region deserves them. Aside from Alaska, the Salmon River flows through the largest roadless area remaining in the forty-eight contiguous United States, nine million acres, twice the size of the state of Massachusetts. We love to bandy about such figures, which really don't mean much, unless we are forced by circumstance to measure them with our bodies. Then, toiling up these mountainsides, around the rocks, through the poison ivy, under the pines and firs, we might begin to comprehend what distance and difficulty really mean and begin to understand what the word *wilderness*, for all its euphonious beauty, actually implies.

Best stick to the river. Despite its forbidding name, the Salmon, River of No Return, makes by far the easiest route to follow through this huge and mountainous wilderness. True, Lewis and Clark turned back. Faced with the rocks and foaming water of the Salmon, they retreated eastward twenty-five miles to the entrance of the Salmon River gorge and turned north toward Montana, seeking an easier, user-friendlier route to the Pacific. But that was in the year 1805; the Lewis and Clark Expedition did not have the technical equipment or the technical knowledge of white-water boating that we possess today.

Who first named it The River of No Return? And why? Nobody seems to know. The resident Shoshone Indians called this river Tom-Agit-Pah, meaning "Big Fish Water," after the Chinook salmon which flourished here, long ago, before the era of dam-building began and the salmon were cut off from their spawning grounds. Probably the name originated among the early fur trappers, prospectors, and miners who were the first whites to explore and attempt to settle this region. They discovered that you could take a boat down this wild and rocky stream; you could not bring it back upstream. It was a one-way journey, and if followed far enough, the Salmon led to the Snake River, the Snake to the Columbia, the Columbia to the Pacific Ocean. "Ocian in view! O joy!" wrote Clark in his journal.

The Salmon is a respectable-sized river, 425 miles long (we are running only a short 90-mile length of it on this trip), dropping eight thousand feet from its alpine sources to its confluence with the Snake, and draining fourteen thousand square miles of mountain country. The Salmon itself is dam-free, but because of the many dams on the Columbia and Snake Rivers, its waters no longer run freely to the ocean.

Nowadays the "No Return" aspect of the Salmon has been modified. An invention called the jet boat makes it possible to travel upstream, as well as down, on this river. We will see several jet boats on our trip, thundering up the river, crashing through the rapids. The jets are used to provide convenient transportation to the several dude ranches along the banks of the Salmon. They are noisy but fast.

The only people who think any more of the Salmon as the river of no return are the tourism operators in a bad year, when they call it the River of No Financial Return. In any case, the river supplied a good name for an old movie, the one starring Marilyn Monroe and some other Hollywood types.

We cruise idly down the placid stream. Yellow pine and mountain mahogany grow right to the riverside. On the lion-colored slopes above the trees I see the paths made by deer, bighorn sheep, and formerly cattle, following the contours of the mountainside. The entire canyon has been subjected to cattle grazing, at one time or another, but because of the immense difficulty of getting their beasts in and out of this rough landscape the ranchers never made money.

We see no cows but do see, soon after put-in, a bighorn ram posing prettily on an outcrop of gray granite. A gratifying sight, the sort of thing we expect Idaho to provide.

There are other animals present, shaded up in the brush, but belonging here: whitetail deer, mountain lion, coyote, bobcat, lynx, beaver, river otter, elk, even moose in the high mountain tarns, and the occasional wandering, carefree black bear. According to the guidebooks, a hundred and twelve species of birds inhabit this region, in one season or another, including bald and golden eagles, ospreys, hawks, falcons, wild turkey, geese, ducks. We won't see many of these creatures on a casual six-day float trip but it's good to know, all the same, that they are out there somewhere, watching us drift past.

And there's fish in the river. No oceangoing salmon any more, but plenty of steelhead and brook trout, rainbow trout, whitefish, smallmouth bass, chubs, suckers, squawfish. I am glad to see that several members of our party have brought their fishing tackle along.

Two miles below our put-in point we encounter the first flurry of white water, a moderate hullabaloo of churning waves, concealed rocks, and noisy waters called Gunbarrel Rapids. The massive Hypalon boats, steered by muscular boatmen, negotiate this obstacle with little difficulty. Those of us in the paddle boat, trying to follow our captain's orders—"Left turn! Right turn! Back paddle, back paddle! Forward!"—ship a little water, take some waves aboard, and get satisfactorily wet and cooled. One of the kids in the inflatable kayaks flips his boat and takes a swim through the waves in his lifejacket but this is a routine and trivial incident, part of the fun. In fact the canyon is so hot—in the nineties—and the water so pleasantly cool that most of us spend half our time in the water by choice.

Why the name Gunbarrel? Somebody, long ago, left his rifle in the crotch of a tree nearby.

We go ashore on a sandy beach for lunch. Cold cuts and cookies, bread, crackers, cheese, fruit, nuts. Cold fruit juice from the water cooler. As always on a river trip, enhanced by hunger, everything tastes good.

I sit on a rock, shielded from the blazing sun by a huge straw hat, and watch the green dark river flow steadily by, smooth as oil, powerful and quiet, unperturbed, and imperturbable. Near me the yellow pines are breathing, and arrays of dazzling sunflowers turn their faces to the light. "Such suchness," as my Zen friends say; a man could easily sink into a permanent trance of meditation here, watching that river coming on, rolling by, surging around the bend below and coming on again. A nation without flowing rivers would be a nation without hope.

I rejoin my friends: the photographer from New York and her three beautiful teenage children, the lawyer from Chicago, the retired defense-plant worker from Oakland, the ex-forester from Washington, all the others. We climb in our boats, push off, float on, rowing and paddling only half the time, watching and listening, and sometimes talking quietly. Something about the solemnity of the river, the silence of the forest, the serene aloofness of the mountains, serves to temper and soften the customary chatter of congregated human beings. I see Cort Conley, old-time river rat, talking to the people in his boat, but although he is only fifty feet beyond I cannot make out a word that he is saying. The general stillness modulates speech, impresses without imposing a kind of natural decorum on everyone.

Two miles beyond Gunbarrel Rapids the river enters a deeper,

more narrow gorge, where it has carved its way through the
great rising mass of uplifted granitic rock called by geologists
the Idaho Batholith. Said to be 100 million years old, this batholith is 250 miles long, 40 to 70 miles wide, trending north
across central Idaho. Our river, running from east to west, has
carved its pathway across and through this structure, a process
of many millions of years. According to the geologists.

Late in the afternoon we run through Devil's Teeth Rapids,
where another passenger falls out of his rubber kayak. He is
salvaged easily, dragged aboard the paddle boat, and the kayak
rescued before it can drift away down the river. We make camp
for the night below the rapid at a place called Devil's Toe Creek.
Our four boatmen build a fire—on an iron firepan, so as not to
pollute the campsite with ashes—and prepare a hearty riverside
dinner: giant tacos with the fixings, topped with a fiery salsa
(optional); salad, soup, fruit juice, coffee (or tea or cocoa), and
for dessert a chocolate cake baked in a Dutch oven.

Some of the passengers pitch their tents, more for the sake
of privacy than for shelter—the sky is clear. Some of us go for
a swim in the big eddy below the rapids. In the hot evening
air of July the river's cool green water feels most refreshing.
Boatman Jeff Wysong uncases his guitar. . . .

Although ours is a brief voyage both in time and space—six
days, ninety miles—the journey settles easily, quickly into a
flow as unhurried and untroubled as that of the river. In the
morning we rise, at various times, and join the boatmen at the
fire for coffee and breakfast and more conversation. Cort Conley, who has made many trips down the Salmon, author of a
book on the river and its people—*River of No Return*—tells
more stories about its history and inhabitants. For him, every
mile of water holds a quota of anecdotes, every ruined cabin
on the banks reminds him of an adventure, a murder, a wed-
ding, a heartbreak, a love affair.

Love: we have a pair of lovers in our party, an inseparable man and woman who cling to one another all day long, whispering in each other's ears, serving each other food and drink. Two young women from San Francisco watch this couple emerging from the woods, late again for mealtime. "My God," says one, "those two are so much in love they even go to the toilet together."

In the sweet cool clear dawn I withdraw to a secluded spot to write my notes for the day. The crew are busy striking camp, loading the boats, policing the kitchen area, and the sight of that labor disturbs my equanimity. Despite my years of lower-middle-class life (ten of them now) I still find it uncomfortable to sit on my rear end while other people work. One solution to my discomfort would be to pitch in and grab ahold; the other is to withdraw. I withdraw.

On the river again. Today I try my hand at the inflatable kayak and run a few rapids in it, including the one called Salmon Falls. The pneumatic vessel oozes nicely over the brawling waves, slides like a salamander over submerged fangs, slips like a weasel between the rocks that rise above the surface. Of course it is only a toy, with little resemblance to a true kayak. Only half decked-over, it ships too much water in every riffle, is impossible to bail, and therefore obliges the paddler to make frequent stops ashore to turn the thing upside down and pour the water out.

We stop at a place called Barth Hot Springs, sit in an open natural pool one hundred feet above the river, and soak for a while in the steamy 134-degree waters that pour from a fissure in the volcanic precipice above. Who was Barth? someone asks Cort Conley. I quote his reply from his book:

The location was known as Guleke Hot Springs for nearly 30 years. Elmer Keith said Cap Guleke used the cabin on the flat. Don Smith remembers a fellow growing rye for whisky there. At the turn of the century there was evidence of extensive placer mining here, including a whip-sawed wooden flume carrying water out of the creek for almost a mile. Chinese miners did some of the early placering. R. G. Bailey said large numbers of elk were using the springs as a lick in 1903. . . . The modern name for the springs is that of Jim Barth, who had the place in the Twenties.

We drift downstream, watching for wildlife, and see a few bighorn sheep, glimpse a few black-tailed mule deer. Not many: now, in the heat of midsummer, most of the big mammals are high in the mountains, above ten thousand feet and timberline, grazing on tundra, buttercups, Rocky Mountain pussytoes, idling away the brief summer among icy lakes and frozen snowbanks.

Paddling close to one of the big boats, I overhear this dialogue: Passenger to boatman: "That Cort Conley knows so many stories about this river; are they all true?" Boatman to passenger: "There's an easy way to tell. Watch him close. If you see his lips moving he's making it up."

Envy again. We all admire Conley. Such a knowledgeable, capable, competent, charming, and soft-spoken man—he reminds me of Gary Cooper. In fact he looks like Gary Cooper. One of these days we're going to run Conley for Congress. Idaho could use a good man in Washington; they haven't had one for a long time.

More rapids. I sit in cold water up to my waist. Not unpleasant in this heat but even so, after hours of it, kind of monotonous. I am content to yield the vulviform kayak to one of the hot-blooded teenagers in our group, her young body wet-suited in baby fat. Kayak paddle whirling, she slithers off over the water to join her young brother, also in a kayak, about half a mile ahead.

Evening shadows, a golden glitter on the river. We make our second camp at a big sand beach on the right bank, under the pine trees and the Douglas fir. Little birds chirp in the darkness among the trees. I think I hear a lazuli bunting, and a hermit thrush, back in the bush, but cannot see them. Downriver from a group of boulders, a river otter cavorts in the waves, its furred glistening body and liquaceous movements sleek as a serpent's. Pursuing the fish? Maybe—and maybe it's engaged in the sheer joy of play.

Beef stroganoff for supper, served on tin plates from an iron pot, preceded and followed by the hors d'oeuvres, soup, salad, drinks, strawberry shortcake, and so forth. It sounds like vulgar gluttony, but on a river trip, under the sun, in the keen air, splashing into and through and out of cold waves that make a strong man cringe—one gets hungry. There seems to be no alternative to eating, much as one might prefer a more ascetic manner of life.

Another day, another boat. Spelling our boatman at the oars, trying to *earn* my lunch, I gaze upstream at the Salmon River canyon, or valley, and think, What is it, exactly, that makes this forested mountain valley different from almost any other that I've seen in the West? After a minute the answer comes: this valley has never been logged. The forest that we see from the Salmon is a virgin forest, too rough and remote for the timber industry to get a handle on by its old techniques. Now the region could be logged, new methods are available, but fortunately and just in time the place was saved by the Wilderness Preservation Act. We Americans have done some things right. I feel less guilty about the meal I plan to devour this evening.

From the landscape beyond to the close at hand: a black and yellow dragonfly lands on my right oar. The insect bears a strange likeness to a helicopter, not the wings but the fuselage, which lacks only a tail rotor to strengthen the mimicry. I shift the oar slightly, the delicate creature takes off, rising straight up, then hovering, exactly like a helicopter.

We run the white-water rapids called Elkhorn and Growler and watch a kayak go bottom-up in the big waves. A routine adventure by this time, nobody hurt or even discouraged. The kayaker climbs back in her kayak and paddles on. We stop to investigate the old Jim Moore place.

In a large meadow of golden hay stand nine log cabins, all built of dressed logs hewn with a broad axe. It looks at first glance like a village, but Moore lived mostly alone here, from 1898 until 1942. According to Conley, he built the extra cabins because he liked to build and because he didn't want to waste the trees that he cut down in clearing the flat for hayfield and gardens. He kept a few cattle on the place, sold beef, hides, and vegetables to the gold miners passing through. He also dealt in moonshine—whiskey and peach brandy. He kept a horse for a watchdog, fed the horse biscuits. The wooden marker on his backyard grave reads, JAS. MOORE. BORN ABOUT 1868, DIED ABOUT APRIL 25, 1942. Round about the golden fields, now the property of the US Forest Service and US citizens, loom the golden mountains covered with meadows and scattered stands of dark green yellow pine. In the heavy summer silence, as I stand brooding over Moore's grave, I hear only the fanatic chirring of locusts, the murmur of the river three hundred feet below and a quarter mile away.

Late afternoon. We make camp at a place called Ground Hog Bar. We eat a splendid supper: T-bone steak, etc. A splendid sunset fills the canyon notch on the west. After dark the boatmen and the passengers play volleyball on the beach, using a net supported by oars and a volleyball illuminated from within by a tiny battery-powered light. The ball looks like a pale-blue full moon as it floats back and forth through the air, impelled, it would seem, by no volition but its own. Eventually, of course, as we all expected and secretly hoped, the volleyball ends up on the river, bobbing down the waves, still glowing like a moon, to disappear around the next bend on the river of no return.

In the heat of the morning sun we stuff faces and stomachs with blueberry pancakes, tubular units of link sausage, cantaloupe melon, several gallons of rich river coffee, then hasten onto the water for relief from the heat and for the delights of more thrashing through the rapids.

I check my bird list: teal, merganser, mallard; raven, kingfisher, golden eagle, and bunting (heard but not seen). Robins everywhere, naturally; they do get around. I've seen robins north of the Arctic Circle, north of the Brooks Range on the bleak and barren North Slope. Such a common, commonplace, prosaic, and plebeian bird—and yet its song is as sweet and beautiful as that of the nightingale I once heard, long ago, in a thicket of trees on a heath—Egdon Heath—in Thomas Hardy's England. And a brave tough little bird. Once on the sands beneath a mesquite tree in Death Valley I saw a big male roadrunner pounce upon a careless robin. There was a whirling tussle, a flurry of feathers—and the robin escaped, flew free into the air. The roadrunner stared after it with his comb erect, beak agape, eyes bulging, the perfect expression of dumbfounded astonishment.

Again today I paddle one of the air-filled kayaks. No one else wants it. Even the teenagers are getting bored with sitting in cold water and swimming too many rapids. But I like it, at least for a few hours. With this quasi-kayak I can speed far ahead beyond the leading boat, enjoying the solitude of the river, stop on shore whenever and wherever I wish, or drop behind the entire procession, linger in the rear watching the others go beyond the bend and imagine myself—I have a good imagination—as one of Lewis and Clark's advance scouts, searching this river for a passage to the sea.

I see a trail switchbacking up the mountainside. I beach the kayak and march upward through the pines for a couple of miles, through the silent forest. The trail dips into a cool, dank, shadowy ravine where a mountain brook tumbles down from ledge to ledge. I kneel on velvet moss, under an ancient shaggy Douglas fir, and dip my cupped hands into the icy water for a drink. The act is like a sacrament; I am performing a familiar ritual. Before drinking I gaze up and around, half expecting to see Cousin Cougar or Brother Bear watching me from the rock above. I do not see them today. But I know they are there. I drink the good water, rise, and turn back down the trail. On a high open point I look down on the river a thousand feet below, see the four big Echo rafts drifting down the teal-blue water, gliding through the white foam of a riffle, following the sunlight dancing on the waves. No voices reach me but I hear the sound of a harmonica from Cort Conley's boat playing an old refrain: "Shall We Gather at the River?"

This afternoon we stop at Five Mile Creek for a visit to the former home of Sylvan Ambrose Hart, alias Buckskin Bill, "Last of the Mountain Men," who died only a few years ago. Born in 1906 in Oklahoma, Hart came to the Salmon River country during the Great Depression of the 1930s, looking for a place where he could live off the land. He found it. For the next forty years he lived his dream, building his house with native materials on the bank of the river, growing and preserving fruit and vegetables, hunting and trapping game, even manufacturing his own knives, rifles, and kitchenware with scrap metals from abandoned gold mines in the area. His little stuccoed house is now occupied by caretakers; Hart's remains are buried on the boundary of his property with his feet, says Conley, extended onto National Forest land, a final act of defiance against a government which had attempted, many times, to evict him from his squatter's homestead.

We camp tonight on a major tributary, the South Fork of the Salmon River. On the large open flats across the river we see a herd of mountain sheep—twenty-one of them, mostly ewes and lambs, with a couple of stately rams standing watch on the crags above the field.

Next morning, as usual, Conley and I are the first ones to rise. We agree that getting up early, before anyone else, gives one a feeling of moral superiority that may last, on a good day, all day long. Furthermore, early morning is the sweetest time of day, any day. That's when your senses are keenest, your mind liveliest, your heart most alive and hopeful.

Others join us, one by one. As we linger near the fire drinking our coffee Conley discourses on the advantages of Idaho, why it is his favorite Western state, his home of choice. He prefers Idaho because of its relatively small human population, the result of several helpful economic vectors: long miserably cold winters; marginal industry; awkward location for shipping and interstate commerce; a poor and stumbling electronics industry; poor transportation systems; too much land "locked up" in official wilderness areas, blocking development; all of these factors adding up to a sluggish growth potential. I agree with him: compared to my own bulging, booming, bursting, burgeoning state of Arizona, the future of Idaho looks clean, bright, free, and hopeful. Maybe I'll move.

Down the river again, through this sylvan vale of deer and trees and crystal side streams still pure enough to drink from direct, I think of the future here, which looks reasonably secure: for generations to come the Salmon River and its tributaries and its great meandering wedge of a canyon will give pleasure to the people and sustenance to its inhabitants.

Such as the otter; we see another otter this morning, rippling through the waves like a sea snake, a twitching fish in its mouth. We see a falcon veering through the sky, only a glimpse, before it disappears into the tall pine. We pass Cougar Creek, Indian Creek, Rabbit Creek, Rugged Creek, Crooked Creek. We pause for an hour at the Shepp Ranch, an elegant and beautifully cared-for guest ranch, where the resident owner, Jim Campbell, a friend of Cort Conley's (Conley knows everybody along this river), gives us two big watermelons from his garden. The watermelons, sweet, cool, juicy, disappear at lunchtime, consumed by twenty-four hungry boaters.

We hike up Crooked Creek a few miles, through the glades of yellow pine, for a look at some small cascades, then return to our watercraft. Onward, into the blazing afternoon, past Basin Creek and Whisky Bob Creek and on to Bull Creek, where we make our final camp of the trip. Storm clouds gather overhead, a wind is rising, and she looks like rain. Some of the passengers hurry to pitch their tents among the sand dunes on the beach. Those tents will not stand long, I think, and sure enough, when the wind comes the tents go down, flapping like bats. The wind is followed by a brief spatter of rain. The sky clears overhead, the sun sinks in a welter of western clouds, and that is the end of the storm.

Italian night: we eat lasagna for dinner, along with an enormous tossed salad, mounds of pan-fried garlic bread, and a jug of California red wine. Brownies for dessert, accompanied by the last circulation of Scotch in a plastic bottle. The singers gather around Jeff Wysong and his guitar. I go for a walk up the trail that follows this river for most of its course, an antique trail built the hard way, by hand labor with pick and shovel and a few mules to carry the tools. Back in the 1930s the CCC

(Civilian Conservation Corps) began a road that was meant to traverse the entire canyon, but this project, interrupted by World War II, was never completed. The trail takes me to a high gray granite crag overlooking the river and the canyon, with a good view of the higher country beyond. I pause there, while the twilight thickens, then pick my way in darkness back to our camp.

Last day on the river. Floating downstream in one of the kayaks, I look through transparent green water and watch the golden rocks rush past beneath. They seem to move with alarming speed, as if the river were approaching a great dropoff, a Niagara where the Salmon vanishes into underground caverns measureless to man. Not so. In fact the river tends to slow before each rapid, forming a pool above the partial dam of boulders. At that point the river pours in a glossy tongue between the largest rocks, suddenly accelerating, and plunges into a frothy circus of colliding waterfalls, suckholes, protruding teeth of stone, whirlpools, recoiling waves. Charging over and through these hazards, if you can, you enter the tail of the rapids, where things start calming a bit, and come out on the smooth water below, still seated inside your boat, you hope, or swimming toward another boat, if necessary.

Gliding through the canyon over water slick as glass, through sunlight and shadow, we watch the rock walls pass by, the clouds floating far above. Following Conley's boat, I find myself thinking of water music. The thought is followed as it was anticipated by the reality: Conley has dug a tape deck from his duffel bag and is playing Handel's *Water Music* as we drift toward our take-out point at Vinegar Creek, only two miles farther. Sunshine and scenery, good company on a free river, great music sounding and resounding from a drifting boat—the queen of England never had it half so good.

Forty Years
as a Canyoneer

*I*n the summer of 1944 a Pennsylvania farm boy, seventeen, about to be drafted into the Army of the United States, hitchhiked around the USA to see for the first time the nation he was being asked to go to war for. Headed east from California, returning home, he took a detour at Williams, Arizona, for the sixty-mile side trip to the South Rim of the Grand Canyon. Traffic was sparse in those wartime days but he managed to hitch a ride. One mile south of the Canyon he had the driver stop and let him out. "But I'm going right on to the Rim," the driver said. "Yes sir," the boy said, "but I think I'd rather walk."

That boy was myself (as I recall) and his reason for wanting to walk the final mile rather than ride may not be easy to explain. It has something to do with what Wordsworth called "natural piety." Even then, in my callow adolescence, it seemed to me somehow disrespectful, even irreverent, even blasphemous to ride to the edge of the Grand Canyon seated on one's backside inside an upholstered, jiggling, clanking, mechanical contraption like the automobile. I preferred to approach the Canyon through the woods, away from the road, mounted on nothing but my own two feet. I wanted to see this great sanctuary of space and form and color as the Indians had seen it, as the Spanish explorers had seen it in the early sixteenth century, as the first Americans had seen it—suddenly. Without official notice.

Keeping the afternoon sun on my left, I walked northeasterly through the ponderosa and jack pine, through the fragrance of the trees, over the matted carpet of pine needles, toward the bright shining openness that waited ahead. I carried a rolled-up blanket slung across my shoulders, like the hobo that I was that summer, a little canvas satchel in one hand, and a canteen of water. I crossed the former road that ran through the woods to the east, walked another half mile, and arrived as I had hoped, *suddenly*, upon the edge of things. The Grand Canyon of the Colorado, no more and no less, lay before me.

I stood a little east of Mather Point, on a part of the South Rim which at that time had not yet suffered the development that was to come. To my right, a mile beyond the Pipe Creek amphitheater, was Yaki Point, and below were the great drop-offs of the Kaibab, Coconino, and Redwall formations, leading eye and mind and heart down, down, down, down to the Tonto Bench, to the Inner Gorge, to the hidden river. Taken all in all, I found it a satisfying spectacle, and if I'd been as naturally pious as one should be at this place, I would have gone down on my knees and meditated in reverent silence. Instead, to tell the truth, the first thing I did was urinate off the rim onto a little aspen tree waiting patiently below. It was a semiconscious act, no offense meant, signifying a claim to territoriality. But I have belonged to the Grand Canyon ever since, possessing and possessed by the spirit of the place.

In the summer of 1949 I camped for five weeks down in a

branch of the Grand Canyon called Havasupai Canyon, now famous for its Indian village and splendid waterfalls, but then little known. Almost unknown. Six years later I took my wife Rita there for a second honeymoon. By the verge of Havasu Falls under the light of a desert moon, quite deliberately, we conceived our first child. In 1961 I worked as a firefighter and fire lookout on the North Rim—among those magic forests and meadows—and did the same in 1968, 1969, and 1970. In 1963 I fell recklessly in love with a girl who lived in Grand Canyon village. (After a summer of passion she left me for another man—her husband.) In 1967 I worked as a river ranger at Lee's Ferry at the head of the Grand Canyon and made the first of several voyages down the Colorado, through the heart of the Canyon (*The* Canyon as its lovers call it) to its terminal necrosis in Lake Merde. Later I wrote a novel about love, death, mystery and—the Grand Canyon. Three years ago I acquired a patch of otherwise utterly worthless rock and sand that overlooks, from high on a cliff, a stretch of the Grand Canyon; I plan to build a secret home there. And in almost every year between 1944 and now I have made at least one descent into the Canyon, often by the classic routes of the Kaibab and Bright Angel Trails, and at other times down secondary, tertiary, primitive pathways, obscure and unreliable, such as the Nankoweap, Boucher, Tanner, and Thunder River. (The last-named trail leads to the world's shortest river: from its source in the caverns called Thunder Springs to its junction with Tapeats Creek and the Colorado, Thunder River is one-half mile long. It is also the only *river* which disappears into a *creek*.)

Because of this long association, spanning four decades with yet more to come, I claim ownership of the Grand Canyon. Not exclusive ownership. I am happy to share with all who come here, whether they approach in the mood of semisolemn reverence, as I did, or like the schoolgirl I saw the other day, stepping onto the terrace of Bright Angel Lodge for the first time in her life, who took one swift glance down into the wonder of the ages, exclaimed "Neat-o!" and returned to the curio shop to buy postcards. The Grand Canyon belongs to all—and to no one. When my own turn comes to lie down, die, and decay, nourishing in the process some higher form of life—a clump of sage, a coyote, a prickly pear, a pissed-on aspen tree—I hope the blessed event takes place high on a canyon rim, with a final vision of red cliffs, magenta buttes, and purple mesas in my fading eyes.

Meanwhile—the great Canyon endures. It was here before humankind was even a twig on the evolutionary tree of life and it will be here when we are gone. The Canyon endures the trifling busyness of humans as it does the industry of ants, the trickle-down erosion of storm and ice, the transient insult of the upstream dams. Those things shall pass, the Canyon will outlive them all.

A humbling thought? Not necessarily. The grandeur of the Canyon confers dignity on every form of life that touches it. Through our love, requited or not, we share in its beauty, power, glory, and sublimity. It is an honor to be a visitor at the Grand Canyon of the Colorado, as it is an honor and a privilege to be alive, however briefly, on this rare, sweet, delicate, one and one only planet we call Earth.

Big Bend

**Delights of
the Approach**

Half the pleasure of a visit
to Big Bend National Park, as in certain other affairs, lies in
the advance upon the object of our desire. Coming toward the
park from the village of Lajitas deep in west Texas, we see this
rampart of volcanic cliffs rising a mile above the surrounding
desert. Like a castled fortification of Wagnerian gods, the Chisos
Mountains stand alone in the morning haze, isolated and for-
midable, unconnected with other mountains, remote from any
major range. Crowned with a forest of juniper, piñon pine, oak,
madrone, and other trees, the Chisos rise like an island of
greenery and life in the midst of the barren, sun-blasted, apparently lifeless, stone-bleak ocean of the Chihuahuan Desert.
An emerald isle in a red sea.

A deception, naturally. Appearances are real but not all that
is real is immediately revealed. The real must be unfolded,
layer by layer. The desert through which we make our ap-

proach, for example, is by no means without life, despite the harsh nakedness of the landscape. Driving up the road from Lajitas and the Rio Grande, we encounter a roadrunner scampering across the highway, followed by a suicidal jackrabbit which my friend Jack Loeffler, at the wheel of the truck, swerves to avoid, followed by a lizard that streaks across the pavement so fast we cannot identify it. In the windy air above a Harris hawk patrols its beat, looking for lunch. The presence of the hawk implies the presence on the ground below, among the desert's scrubby vegetation, of a fair population of mice, rabbits, ground squirrels, lizards, and other reptiles. Beyond the hawk, and common everywhere in the Big Bend area, soars the red-headed turkey vulture—sometimes in swarms. Where life is there is death, reasons the vulture, and where there's death there's hope. When life is cheap death is rich.

But it's that magic island mountain in the center of the scene that holds our eyes. We bear straight toward it, eager to escape the mid-September heat of the desert, if only for a few hours. At Lajitas, two thousand feet above sea level, the thermometer at noon read 102 degrees Fahrenheit. One hundred two in the shade—and away from the village there is no shade. Not a tree in sight down here in the badlands but a few little thorny mesquites, about waist-high to a man, struggling for survival in the stony ravines that lead to the river.

We pass the old mining town of Terlingua, a cluster of stone and adobe buildings, most in ruins. When I first saw Terlingua back in the fifties it was a true ghost town, uninhabited by humans. Now a few of the better buildings have been renovated and the largest serves as store, post office, and headquarters of a river-running outfit calling itself Far-Flung Adventures, Inc. For a fair and reasonable fee the young men and women of Far-Flung will take you by canoe, kayak, or rubber raft through the whirling rapids and fifteen-hundred-foot-deep gorge of nearby

Santa Elena Canyon, a pleasant three- or four-day outing which I myself have enjoyed twice. The name Terlingua is said to be a corruption of the Spanish *tres linguas*—three languages. The three languages once spoken in this area, which gave the town its name, would have been Spanish, English, and probably Comanche. Spanish and English remain in use here—the Mexican border is only a few miles away—but the Comanches are long gone.

But not forgotten. That newly risen moon, three-quarters full, floating on the eastern sky, was once called "Comanche moon," a sight sufficient to inspire terror in the hearts of many a Mexican villager during the seventeenth and eighteenth centuries. For it was at this time of year, by the light of the first autumn moon, that the nomadic Comanches would leave their prairie home, leave the buffalo, and turn their horses south for the annual raid into northern Mexico. Traveling in large bands by night, resting during the heat of the day, the Comanche warriors rode south sometimes as far as Durango, pillaging, burning, killing all the way. The Mexicans, scattered across a vast region in small towns and isolated ranches, were powerless to do much more than send out parties of militiamen in futile pursuit. Not until the Americans conquered Texas during the first half of the nineteenth century, destroying the great buffalo herds that formed the energy basis of the Comanche way of life, was this fierce proud tribe starved into submission and herded onto the Oklahoma reservations.

We have good reason to think of frontier history as we drive steadily toward the looming mass of the Chisos Mountains. Not only is the Comanche moon hanging in the sky—pale wafer in the sunlight—we are also intersecting one of the major north-south routes of those vanished raiders, whose annual migration took them through the middle of what is now Big Bend National Park. Following these same tracks for centuries, the Indians left in their course so many skeletons of stolen cattle, horses, and human captives that their path became known as the Trail of Bones. Nothing can be seen of this trail any more; the white bones of the Comanches' victims have had 130 years to disintegrate and disappear.

Green Gulch: Ascent to the Island in the Desert

Our road rises fast as we come close to the mountains, from two thousand feet at Lajitas on the Rio Grande to four thousand feet at the turnoff for the Chisos Basin. Here we leave the burnt-out badlands of the desert for the piñon-juniper forest above, following Green Gulch, the sole feasible auto route into the center of the mountains. All other approaches are ruled out by the vertical walls of rock that give the Chisos their fortresslike appearance.

Green Gulch is a broad valley of trees, fields, and grasses lined by the red and gray cliffs of the mountain, the road climbing steeply toward Panther Pass. The valley narrows; we pass a couple of watering stations for overheated engines. At the seven-thousand-foot mark we reach the saddle of the ridge and descend into the Chisos Basin.

The Basin resembles a cup in the hills, a craterlike depression three miles in diameter, its lowest point two thousand feet below the surrounding ring of peaks. Not volcanic, the Basin resulted from natural erosion processes carried out over the usual geological time scales—in this case, the millions of years that have elapsed since the Cenozoic Era.

The Basin is well-wooded in trees characteristic of higher elevations in the west Texas region: one-seed juniper, drooping juniper, alligator juniper (so named for the checkered scales of its bark), Mexican piñon pine, the Texas madrone, and various kinds of oaks such as the Emory and the Graves. Higher in the hills, in deep and shaded canyons, are groves of Ponderosa pine, some Douglas fir, and the southernmost glades of quaking aspen in the entire United States.

My friend Jack and I eat a late lunch at a shady table in the public campground. Although this is a weekday in mid-September, well after the end of the summer tourist season and too early for the winter season, the campground is half full. We check out the stables, the store, have a look at the lodge, then fill our canteens and walk the easy two miles that lead to a great stone notch on the west side of the Basin—an opening in the encircling rim of hills appropriately called the Window.

Through the Window we enjoy a grand view of the jumble of mesas, buttes, pinnacles, canyons, and volcanic plugs that form the western side of Big Bend. The multicolored landscape stretches away toward isolated peaks of barren rock with names like Study Butte, Contrabando Mountain, Rattlesnake Mountain, Maverick Mountain, Cigar Mountain, Indian Head, Fossil Knobs, and Hen Egg, topped off by a remote, mysterious, laccolithic dome called El Solitario.

The Window itself forms the outlet for the entire drainage system of the Basin. There is no surface water here (most of the time), the gullies and ravines are generally bone dry, but when it does rain, and sometimes it does, all of the water not absorbed by the ground funnels out through the twenty-foot-wide notch at the bottom of the Window. This well-polished little gorge leads to the seventy-five-foot drop of the "pouroff," as Texans call such places, the spout at the end of the tilted gravy bowl.

As we stand there admiring the view of the hot red desert below, a hawk takes off from a nearby bigtooth maple, lumbering heavily into the air. Swainson's! says I. No, says Jack. I guess again: Marsh? Rough-legged? Bow-legged? No, he says, look. The hawk has sailed through the notch of the waterless pouroff and soars on the rising thermals beyond the cliffs. But the descent here is so great, hundreds of feet down, and so precipitous, that this hawk, though indeed soaring, is soaring *beneath* us. We look down upon its dark brown back and wings, its rust-red and fan-shaped buteo tail. Just another red-tailed hawk, imperially beautiful and as common as the turkey buzzard.

A Jewel in the Stone

The campground, as I've said, is only half full. But that means only half empty. For Jack and me that's not enough; we want to camp in the outback for chrissake, the primitive country, the wild—what else is a national park for? If we wanted human company we'd go to Attica, San Quentin, Bellevue. And so, when the worst of the afternoon heat is over, we climb into the old pickup, drive out of the Basin, descend Green Gulch and return to the simmering inferno of the desert. Hot indeed, but the sun is low in the west and the cool of evening will soon be here, illuminated by the waxing Comanche moon. We pause at Panther Junction (Park headquarters) to fill our water jugs and obtain a back-country camping permit (you thought this was a free country?), then roll down the long slope of the land toward the Rio Grande and the southeast corner of the Big Bend.

Jack has a certain campsite in mind, a place I've never got around to in my previous visits here. He points to a dun-colored ridge in the east. Out there, he says. The area looks completely devoid of interest from the highway—drab, dull, desolate— but that ridge, sure enough, proves to be our destination. We cross a bridge over a broad river of sand, take a rough dirt road through the rocks past endless fields of lechuguilla (a kind of

agave popularly known as "shin-dagger"), creosote bush, oco-
tillo (a species alone unto itself), and various families of prickly
pear and barrel cactus. Negotiating with care the axle-busting
trenches that transect the road, we take a secret turnoff point
to a dead-end in a sand-filled arroyo. We halt. Half a mile up
the sandy wash is a deep, narrow, dark cleft winding into the
limestone ridge.

We make our camp as the sun goes down, the near-full moon
shining overhead. A fine desert evening, the air clear and warm,
with the stillness unbroken by any sound but that of a few
insects, the evening breeze through the acacia, the first warm-
up cries of a poorwill.

After eating a hasty supper—eager to go exploring—we march
up the sandy floor of the draw and into the mouth of the cleft
in the ridge. The cleft reveals itself as a canyon of respectable
dimensions, perhaps five hundred feet deep and of indeter-
minate length, for we fail to get to the upper end of it. It is
also a place of considerable beauty, with winding and overhanging walls, a gothically crenellated rim, and a pleasingly
eroded limestone floor. The most delightful feature is a series
of natural stone tanks in the blue-gray stone of the creekbed.
Most of these tanks, or potholes, or *tinajas*, as the Spanish
called them, are partially filled with water, and one looks so
appealing that we cannot resist the temptation to go for a swim.
The water is neck-deep and cool, the bottom firm with coarse
gravel and sand. We share the pool with tadpoles, mosquito
larvae, a few black and yellow waterbugs of the type called
"boatmen," and one small green garter snake. As we step into
the water the snake wriggles over the surface and eases into a
rock slit on the opposite side. One final flick of tail and the
snake disappears. We name the place Garter Snake Tank.

Returning to camp, we pass a larger tank filled with water
so deep it looks black, opaque as obsidian. Below is a growth

of cane or bulrushes, suggesting permanent water. In the wet sand we identify the heartshaped hoofprints of whitetail deer and javelina. Also present, indicated by their autographs, is the customary desert assortment of lizards, beetles, side-winding rattlesnakes, quail, doves, and jackrabbits.

We go to sleep to the music of a single lonesome poorwill and from much farther away, up among the dark crags of the canyon, the soft but insistent hoot of an owl. What kind of owl? To me it sounds like a great horned owl. But Jack Loeffler, who knows, identifies the call as that of the "flammulated owl." (*Flammulated?* A likely story. "Flammulated owl" suggests pixilated companion.)

Black Gap and the River Road: Fifty Miles of Hell on Wheels

The rising sun drives us up and early out of camp. We head back toward the mountains, thinking of the cool high-elevation air, but stop for a brief visit to the little oasis of Dugout Wells. Here a group of bright green cottonwood trees and a jungle of other water-loving plants like willow and tamarisk cluster around a derelict windmill and a seep of water. Lingering in the shade, we reconsider our plans for the day and decide—what the hell— to forsake the mountains and plunge instead across the painted badlands and through the summertime inferno that lies between the mountains and the Rio Grande. Leaving the highway, we take the primitive trail-road southeast for Chilicotal Mountain, Glenn Springs, Black Gap, and the River Road.

We've both driven part of this route before and know very well that it's a primitive byway, rough and lonesome. Jack's truck, however, is equipped with heavy-duty transmission and compound low (creeper or granny) gear; we're stocked up on water and food; and most important—we want to do it. There are things in Texas worse than a mere fifty miles of rock and sand. I'd rather be broke down and lost in the wilds of Big Bend, any day, than wake up some morning in a penthouse suite high above the megalomania of Dallas or Houston.

Crawling over the jagged stones at an average speed of five to ten miles per hour, we admire at leisure the ramparts of the Chisos on our right, soft gold and rosy red in the late morning sunlight—Nugent Mountain, Panther Peak, Casa Grande, Crown Mountain, and beyond these, the sheer escarpment of the South Rim. (Tomorrow I'll be up there looking down.) On our left and ahead is Chilicotal Mountain, Talley Mountain, the anticline called Cow Heaven, and about fifteen miles away the monocline of Mariscal Mountain. Anticline, syncline, monocline: Big Bend is a playground not only for tourists like us but also for rock-happy geomorphologists.

We stop often for relief from the jouncing ride and for a good look-around at the exhilarating panorama of desert mountains, especially the grand façade of the Sierra del Carmen across the river in Mexico. The highest parts of that range, forty miles away by airline, rise to nine thousand feet above sea level. Someday we'll get there too.

Reluctantly we pass the turnoffs for Pine Canyon and Juniper Canyon but find time to stop for lunch, a beer, and a walk at the ruins of old Glenn Springs, another desert swamp of phreatophytes clustered around a buried water source. Below the spring a stream of clear water trickles over rocky ledges; on higher ground nearby are traces of human history, the remains of stone walls, piles of rusty tin cans, muleshoes and horseshoes—all that remains of the hundreds of years of Indian, Mexican, and American encampments that once existed here.

The road forks at Glenn Springs. The left-hand fork goes southeast to the eastern end of the River Road, the right-hand fork southwest through Black Gap to join River Road near Cow

Heaven anticline. The left-hand fork is passable, we know, to motor vehicles with high clearance and short wheelbase, but the right-hand fork, according to the Park Service warning sign, is FOUR-WHEEL DRIVE ONLY. Furthermore, states the notice, ROAD IS ROUGH, INFREQUENTLY PATROLLED, TOWING CHARGES ARE HIGH. We interpret this malarkey as a challenge and head off for Cow Heaven by the Black Gap cutoff.

We discover that the sign deserves consideration. At several places we find it necessary to halt and reconnoiter, remove boulders, bevel off cutbanks with a shovel, and drive the truck astraddle over some potentially fatal gullies down the centerline of the roadway. The Black Gap itself turns out to be a steeply ascending, very narrow gulch blasted through volcanic bedrock, leaving a surface of staircase ledges studded with rock teeth capable of puncturing fuel tank, oil pan, or equanimity. I lead the way on foot, walking backward, guiding Jack at the wheel by hand signals over and through the worst hazards. The descent on the other side of the ridge is even hairier; we'd never get the truck back up this.

Fortunately a return is not necessary. After two hours of slow but interesting work we arrive at the junction with River Road. Only thirty miles of sandy washes, gravel gulches, and rocky flats remain between us and the old village of Castolon at the west end of our route. We celebrate with cold beer and proceed, observed from above and afar by the usual escort of hopeful vultures.

We pass a side road leading down to the river, four miles to the south. The heat is intense, an absorbing preoccupation, but we have determined to get as far as a place called Reed Camp, where the road skirts the banks of the Rio Grande, before going in for a swim. On the way we round the south end of Cow Heaven anticline, a low-lying structure of great interest to geologists but less picturesque than its name. Beyond, however, rise the eerie forms of Elephant Tusk, Dominguez Mountain, Mule Ear Peaks, Punta de la Sierra, and the main mass of the Chisos Mountains—a romantic jumble of volcanic plugs, intrusive laccoliths, extrusive buttes, and the stratified formations of ancient lava flows.

Our road enters thick stands of mesquite and tamarisk in the flood plain of the river. The growth is so dense that it would be difficult to beat a path through to the water. We drive on and, a little farther, about to cross a wide arroyo of sand and baked mud, we see the river at the mouth of the drainage, only thirty yards away on our left. We park the truck in what shade is available and wade into the Rio Grande wearing only our hats. The river is low, the water shallow; we sit on the shifting sands of the riverbed, bracing our heels against the tug of the current, and watch the best brown topsoils of Texas, New Mexico, and Chihuahua floating seaward past our chins.

A hundred feet away, across the swirling brown waters, is another jungle of tamarisk, willow, and clumps of tall white-headed cane (the giant reed, *Arundo donax*). That jungle is the northern frontier of the Republic of Mexico, State of Coahuila. A few rack-ribbed, hungry, Mexican scrub cattle stare at us from their shady tunnels in the thicket, waiting a chance to sneak across the river into the far better forage on the US side of the border. Having denuded their own range, they now lust after ours.

Jack and I idle away a couple of hours in and near the river, waiting out the worst heat of the afternoon and guarding our national heritage from unwelcome intruders. One final dip in the water and then, refreshed, we drive on toward the west.

To be halted shortly by a wooden barricade. ROAD CLOSED, says the sign. We get out to investigate. The road ahead lies across a mudbank on the outside bend of the river; the bank is undercut, with tricky-looking cracks fissuring the roadway. The road appears to be on the verge of collapsing into the Rio Grande at any moment; on the other hand it may stand for hours or maybe even a few more days. We set the barricade aside for a minute and drive on through to firm ground, stop, walk back, and return it to its place. The fact that we got safely past should not encourage others. We made it; the next may not.

Jack drives down a ten-foot mudbank into a ravine and climbs with difficulty up the far side. I remove another barricade from our path, we drive forward, replace the barricade, and continue. Late in the afternoon we come to a grand and open place high on a ridge. We stop, camp for the night. To the west we can see the slot in the mountain where the Rio Grande has carved Santa Elena Canyon the deep underworld of Mesa de Anguila. (Mountain of eagles? The name is of uncertain origin, ambiguous meaning.) Below, four or five miles away, flickering through the gloom, are the lights of the village of Castolon, where the River Road rejoins the paved park highway. We have come through, daunted but undamaged. Pleased by everything around us, we honor the occasion with a ceremonial supper of tortillas, cheese, refried beans—burritos à la Mex-Tex—and ease our passage into sleep with nightcaps of cocoa laced by liberal splashes of Wild Turkey.

Last Day: A Walk on the Rim

One thirty P.M.: Rather late in the day to be starting a fourteen-mile hike but I have no choice. Jack must start back to Santa Fe tomorrow—a seven-hundred-mile drive—and therefore I must hike the South Rim Trail today. Why? Because I want to; it's now or maybe never. We'd spent the first half of the day at Castolon, investigated the mouth of Santa Elena Canyon, then driven up here into the Chisos Basin one more time for my walk in the woods.

With two quarts of water on my belt and a little bread and cheese in my daypack, I leave the Basin trailhead for the switch-backing climb to Laguna Meadow and the South Rim of the Chisos Mountains. Jack, nursing an injured foot, stays with his truck. The sun blazes down as I climb but there are clouds gathering in the sky; an afternoon storm, in this heat, would be welcome. I'll want a clear and starry sky, though, for the return after dark.

The trail is a horse trail with an easy grade, well maintained. I pass one hiker coming down and two men on horseback; for the rest of the day and evening I will see no one. I trudge through the midget forest of madrone, piñon pine, juniper, and oak. Two thousand feet above the trailhead is Laguna Meadow, a small-scale replica of the Chisos Basin, pleasantly upholstered with tall grasses, shaded by thickets of oak and alligator juniper. A pleasant place in the sunshine, one would like to linger, but the wind is rising, the clouds convocating, and I've about eleven miles yet to walk. I go on, climbing another three miles and five hundred feet to the treeless escarpment of South Rim. I sit on the flat, sedimentary rocks below the edge, out of the wind, air my sweat-soaked shirt, drink a pint of water, eat my lunch, and gaze outward—southwest, south, southeast—over the geological wonderland that Jack and I had wandered through by jeep road yesterday.

The rim drops off straight for a hundred feet, then descends stepwise into the complex of ridges, canyons, buttes, peaks, and mesas below. The Rio Grande, a mile lower and fifteen miles away by line of sight, meanders through its profound canyons. Beyond are the blue-hazed ranges of Old Mexico.

My sun is gone, buried in a mass of black clouds. I'd love to see a storm from up here, watch lightning blast the battlements of Tortuga Mountain, see a flash flood boiling down Smoke Creek Canyon, but—the afternoon is getting on. Reluctantly I bestir myself, resume shirt and pack, and hasten along the Rim Trail, following it for several miles to what is called the East Rim. There I pause for a good final look at the Sierra del Carmen, the Sierra del Caballo Muerto (Dead Horse Mountains), Boquillas Canyon, and the depths of Juniper and Pine Canyons below my feet.

From here the trail leads downward into the forests of Boot Canyon, where the Park Service maintains a cabin near the fairly reliable water of Boot Spring. This is the most lushly forested area in Big Bend, home to ponderosa pine, Douglas fir, and the tall and stately Arizona cypress (also a conifer). I see a few Mexican jays and other birds but catch no sight of that *rara avis* the Colima warbler, a gray and yellowish sparrow-sized bird found nowhere else within the United States. Maybe I'm too late, maybe the Colimas have left already for their winter home in Mexico, and maybe I don't give a damn anyhow: I didn't hike fourteen miles to glimpse a lousy little warbler.

Deep twilight. A few raindrops patter on my sombrero. Above, solid overcast. Not a star or moon to be seen. I pass the trail for Juniper Canyon, another that goes up to Emory Peak, high point of the Park, 7,835 feet above sea level. I was up there once, years before. Once was enough. I hurry on toward Pinnacle Pass and the long descent to road and campground in the Chisos Basin. Through the rain and darkness I note a tall volcanic spire, *erectus majesticus*, at the junction of Boot Canyon and Juniper Canyon. The spire resembles a cowboy's workshoe standing on its pull tabs—the Boot.

Over the pass and down. The trail descends in tight switchbacks, easy to follow even in the dark but littered with loose stones. Would be most inconvenient now to twist an ankle, tear a meniscus, or fall on my face. I proceed with care, feeling my way, remembering that Jack had offered me his flashlight when I departed the trailhead five hours earlier. Won't need it, I assured him. Don't need it, either, I think, feeling my way through the dense gloom under the trees, but—*sure could use it*. A thousand feet below and still two or three miles away by trail, the bright lights of the lodge, the moving beams of automobiles, glare in my eyes. No concern: if I lose the trail I'll simply go down by the fall line, sliding from tree to tree, through clumps of cactus and nests of aggravated rattlesnakes, until I end up, as I must, in the bottom of the Basin.

It's not that hard. My feet keep to the trail even when I cannot see it; an hour later I'm at the lodge. Jack and I drive out of the mountains and make camp at a place called Grapevine Hills, pitching a tent in the light rain. Once the tent is up the rain stops, as usual, and we sleep in the open under a clouded but unleaking sky.

We wake at dawn to discover the desert hills shrouded in rolling clouds of vapor, seeming remote and mystical as the Mountains of the Moon. A rare and lovely sight and we are sorry to leave. We console ourselves, as we always do, with the thought that we'll be back, someday soon. We will return, someday, and when we do the gritty splendor and the complicated grandeur of Big Bend will still be here. Waiting for us. Isn't that what we always think as we hurry on, rushing toward the inane infinity of our unnameable desires? Isn't that what we always say?

TV Show

Out There in the Rocks

(Opening shot of a pretty scene at Arches National Park, Utah. Red sandstone monoliths, blue sky with clouds, call of ravens, silence, sound of distant thunder. Long shot of a car or pickup truck advancing up a dusty, rocky road among junipers and stone—the original entrance road to Arches National Park. We hear the voice of the Old Ranger . . .)

When I first came to the Arches country in 1955, this was the road you entered by. Eight miles of dust and sand and stone. Axle-busting ruts. Tire-blowing rocks. And when it rained, as it sometimes did—often several times a year—then you might bog down in wheel-sucking muck.

(A view of the ruts, the rocks, the sands of Courthouse Wash.)

I loved it. Loved it all. The miserable road, the dust, the wind, the flash floods and the quicksand, the hoodoo monuments and the voodoo arches, the space, the silence, the ravens and vultures and rattlesnakes.

(Appropriate shots of items named. Then a view of the narrator standing on a ridge about half a mile west of Balanced Rock.)

Of course I was paid to love this place. I was a park ranger in those days. I worked here. I was the only ranger in the world who lived in Arches National Park. Right near this spot was my entrance station: a map and a few photographs on a signboard. A registration sheet for visitors to sign. Part of my job was to sit here in the shade, on a folding chair like this, and answer questions, in case a tourist might show up.

(The narrator assumes a rangerlike pose on a chair.)

Sometimes one did. Usually on a Sunday. That was our busy day, Sunday. The questions were always the same. Where the devil are we? and How the hell do we get out of here? I did my best to be helpful. The government paid me $3.50 an hour to be helpful.

(Standing and pointing.)

I lived right down there, in a little plywood housetrailer under a brush ramada. There was a hole in the floor of the trailer so that snakes could get in and out. I worked and lived out here for two years. Wrote a book about it, the first book anybody ever wrote about the Arches. Maybe the last. Later on the government hauled my trailer away to the garbage pit and made this spot a road maintenance supply depot, as you see. They named it the Edward Abbey Memorial Gravel Dump. When I die, if I live that long, I hope to be buried under that pile of gravel.

(Walking near and under the Balanced Rock. View of La Sal Mountains in background. With snow, we hope.)

This was our campground, back in the fifties. There was a bare spot on the ground, about here, for parking your car. Or hobbling your horse. We had room for three cars or six horses. Over there, under those juniper trees, we had a couple of picnic tables. Free-standing picnic tables; you could move them around to follow the shade. Nobody stole picnic tables in those days, I'm not sure why. It was a primitive period in America. Over there, on the southeast side of that phallic object—Entrada sandstone member—was the restroom facility. The comfort station was a little wooden outhouse built over a hole in the ground. A pit toilet. The US government supplied the structure, the hole and the toilet paper, free of charge. There was no water out here, of course. Campers brought their own water. Everybody assumed, in those days, that if you wanted to camp out in the desert you should probably carry water—and beer. We thought that's what the desert was for: a place to invert beercans on a Sunday afternoon. And a place to take water to. Now . . .

(Views of the new entrance station at park headquarters, the new visitor center, the vast black asphalt parking lot, the new ranger residences.)

. . . things have greatly improved. See for yourself. Paved road. A box office—no more of that socialistic free admission business; you buy a ticket or you don't get in. Room for a hundred cars. Two hundred. A modern visitor center with modern restrooms . . .

(Sound of toilets flushing.)

. . . information counter with a clerk always on duty, and a complete museum. Four walls, a roof, a tile floor, central heat-ing, central cooling. You can learn all about the arches now without having to actually see one. And look there: the rangers live in houses, real houses, in their own little ranger village, where they can keep an eye on each other and on their ranger wives. Nowadays a park ranger lives just like anybody else. If these people were suddenly transferred to the suburbs of Phoenix, San Diego, Houston, Atlanta, Long Island, they'd hardly notice any difference.

(*Old Ranger at wheel of rusty red 1970 Olds convertible—* FOR SALE—*racing at sixty-five miles per hour into the park on the new paved road.*)

It used to take a whole day to get in and out of this godawful place. Now anyone with a car in good working order can do it in two hours.

(*Scenes of sandstone pillars, arches, slickrock domes, etc., flashing past.*)

Great views through the windshield. You don't even have to slow down.

(*Oncoming car rushes past with howling horn. Collision narrowly averted.*)

Well, maybe a little. That there's the road over to the Double Arch and the Window Arches. Used to be, you had to walk into there on a little rocky footpath. Took half the day. Now you can buzz in and out in half an hour.

(*Passing a road junction. And another. And a third.*)

That's the road to Delicate Arch. Don't have time to go there right now. Maybe later.

That's the road to Fiery Furnace. I think. Was. Maybe next time.

(*Entering Devil's Garden and the official campground.*)

Now we're back in civilization. Thank God. Notice the ample parking space. The convenient modern restrooms.

(*Shot of water tanker off-loading water.*)

The reliable water supply. There's a million-dollar two-hundred-foot well around here someplace but the pump breaks down now and then. James Watt was gonna fix that but he didn't get around to it. He did have a chlorinator installed, though. The water here was one-hundred-percent pure but people thought it tasted funny—no chlorine flavor. Watt fixed that; now the water here tastes the same as water in Newark, New Jersey or Landfill, Illinois.

(*Shot of campers washing hair under No Washing sign.*)

Now we have plenty of water and it tastes right.

(*Shot of camper—or Old Ranger—gaping over the No Wood Gathering sign.*)

No wool gathering, please.

(*Shot of pretty young woman in tight shorts, bending to pick something up from ground.*)

Always pick up litter. Or whatever. Never leave gum wrappers or condoms lying around on the ground. Give a hoot.

(*Sound of coyote howling. Pause. View of deer passing through field near campground.*)

More sightseers. And . . .

(*Woman alone inside motor home, staring out through the windshield at scene beyond.*)

. . . a contemplator. Why do people come to a place like this? For the solitude and quiet?

(*A couple of cars roar by on the campground road.*)

For the modern facilities?

(*Old woman washing her coffeepot at the No Washing tap.*)

Or for adventure?

(*Shot of small boy clambering over a sandstone dome.*)

Or for something else?

(*Shot of pilgrims trudging up the long slickrock trail toward Delicate Arch. Booted feet. Woman with child, stroller, and bottle of orange soda. A young couple in the wind, their hair blowing.*)

What are we doing here? I don't know either. Just a bunch of ordinary people having a pleasant time in a kind of extra-ordinary place. Except that I don't know any ordinary people. I've never met an ordinary person in my life. But here we are anyhow. Hiking up this mile of bare-naked stone. One huge rock, all in one piece. What's there to do up here? I don't know. Not much.

(*More scenic views: sun on edge of rock. A few juniper trees. Approaching Delicate Arch, we see some of the graffiti on the rock:* Jerry & Sam *and* B.P. '65.)

Well I'm glad to see old Jerry and Sam came by. And old Bill Peterson. What were you fellas doing here?

(*First view of Delicate Arch, children playing on the slick-rock, mountains and mesas beyond.*)

I see.

(Sound of ravens again, and distant thunder.)

The Delicate Arch, they call it. Not as delicate as it looks. Hasn't changed much, so far as I can tell, since 1955, first time I saw it. Hasn't changed at all. That thing may stand for another hundred years. Or for five thousand years. Or fall tomorrow. It doesn't matter. The rock will still be here. The rock and the canyons and the mesas and those mountains over yonder, they'll be around for a million years.

(More views of the scenery: sky, mountains, golden sandstone, domes, clouds, sunlight . . .)

There are some places so beautiful they can make a grown man break down and weep. I should know. But what the hell, the natural world is beautiful everywhere, from the sand dunes of Cape Cod to the sand dunes of Baja California. This rockpile in Utah is special for me mainly because this is part of my home. I live here.

(Shot of Old Ranger walking along near Balanced Rock.)

Arches National Park has changed some since I worked here. Lots more roads now. Plenty of asphalt. Of course, asphalt is beautiful too, in a way. If you like asphalt.

(He stops at edge of paved park road, looks both ways, crosses hurriedly as more cars scream by.)

Awful lot of traffic. Awful lot of people out here in the wilds. Awful lot of people everywhere; that's the kind of world we live in now. You get used to it, I guess. If you have to. But I'm not worried about it much. Nature will take care of things in her same old way, sooner or later. You know: famine, plague, war. The usual. Nobody lives forever. Neither do civilizations. They come and they go, like you and me. That doesn't bother me either.

(He stops and looks up at the Balanced Rock, at the scene beyond.)

I'll tell you what I do wonder about. Here's what really puzzles me . . .

(As the narrator continues, he slowly dissolves before the eye of the camera, fading away into nothing and into silence . . .)

. . . I mean, what will it be like out here when I'm gone and you are gone and our great-grandchildren are gone and even the State of Utah, even America, even this whole big hog heaven of a mechanical civilization is gone? What then? What'll be happening out here when us humans are all gone and forgotten and faded away to nothing . . . ? What then?

(Final shot of the golden rocks, the mesa, the mountains, the clouded sky. Sound of ravens. Sound of thunder.)

Round River Rendezvous

The Rio Grande

OCTOBER 1984

Why not begin at the end?
I stand on the hot sand of the beach and watch the Rio Grande
merge its thick, sluggish, algae-green water with the bright
blue of the Gulf of Mexico. This is Boca Chica (Little Mouth)
and here, near Brownsville, Texas, one of the great American
rivers finally completes its journey to the sea. Barely makes it.
The water seems not to move at all, as if worn out, exhausted
by its 1,885-mile descent from the San Juan Mountains of Colorado, through the canyons of New Mexico and Texas, over and
through dozens of dams, diverted, processed, recycled, all vigor
spent, until at the end the river is little more than a warm,
slow, catfish creek, twenty feet wide and only waist-deep.

The river is not as dead as it looks. Dozens of fishermen wade
in and out of the gentle surf on either side of the Rio Grande's
little mouth. With long poles and heavy lines baited with *cama-
rones*—shrimp—they are seeking their supper. One man
opens his ice box to show me his catch: three whiting and two
five-pound red snappers.

Why are the fishermen clustered here at the mouth of the river? Because the effluents from upstream, the sewage and fertilizers and garbage from towns and farms, attract the hierarchies of small organisms, including shrimp, that attract in turn the large game fish that attract human predators.

Although this is a weekday afternoon, whole families are here. Wives and mothers sit in the shade of battered automobiles and sea-rusted pickup trucks, watching their men. Children play in the firm sand at the water's edge and in the high dunes behind the beach. All but myself appear to be Mexicans, or Mexican-Americans. Here on the international boundary, in this neutral zone, one's actual citizenship makes little difference. The uniformed police of the US Border Patrol are nowhere in sight.

The air is soft, warm, humid, semitropical. It feels to me like potential hurricane weather, but today the sky is clear except for a few small clouds out over the rim of the sea. Sandpipers scurry along the edge of the surf; a few terns fly above, occasionally diving straight down into the water to emerge, a moment later, with or without their prey. Like the men, the terns are fishing.

An old lighthouse stands on the Mexican side of the river's mouth. Hard to believe now, but only a few decades ago the Rio Grande was navigable for almost two hundred miles upstream. In the other direction, northeast, I can see huge resort hotels and condominium towers under construction on the south tip of Padre Island. Boca Chica, however, is still uninhabited— at least for now.

I drive a mile up the hard, damp beach and go for a swim, wading a hundred yards from shore (thinking about stingrays and sharks) before the tepid water becomes chest deep. I float on my back under the hot sun, letting the waves roll over me, and think about the other end of the Rio Grande, the beginning.

Only two weeks earlier my wife and I had been camping at

Stony Pass, nearly thirteen thousand feet above sea level, under green-gold aspen and shaggy spruce, deep in the San Juan Mountains above the mining town of Creede, Colorado. We intended to find the origins of the Rio Grande, the source. *La Source*: I envisioned a mythological maiden in a flowing, diaphanous gown, pouring crystal clear Rocky Mountain spring-water from a jug on her shoulder. What we really found was something much finer.

After my swim I drive back to Brownsville and walk across the international bridge over the Rio Grande to the Mexican town of Matamoros. Unmuffled tanker trucks (hauling drinking water, I am told) thunder across the bridge from Texas into Mexico. The Mexicans, it seems, are having problems with their water supply again. Matamoros, far off the main travel routes, is a fairly presentable place, unlike most border towns. I notice a few leaking sewer lines, a few shoeshine boys, and little girls selling chewing gum. The general appearance of homes and public buildings is one of genteel decay, shaded by date palms and brightened by the red flowers of bougainvillea.

The worst sleaze is on the American side of the border in downtown Brownsville, among the bars, go-go joints, and block after block of little clothing stores. Here I see one of the saddest things I've ever seen, anywhere. Inside a shop labeled *Ropas Usadas* (Used Clothes), a dozen weary little Mexican women, all pregnant, sit among mountains of old clothing, each woman patiently sorting through these trash piles in search of children's garments and stacking her selections in a small heap at her feet. Both temperature and humidity are in the nineties. The air in the place is stifling, swarming with flies, and dense with the unmistakable, unforgettable smell of poverty. The manager of this pen, a swarthy, greasy-haired, crossbred, snake-eyed *bandito*, the only male in view, waits in the corner for the women to finish their sorting and hand over their faded paper pesos.

Hordes of children play outside on the slime and broken glass of the street.

Watching this intolerable, unacceptable scene, which nevertheless we tolerate and accept, I think again of Stony Pass in the San Juans, the clear, cold mountain air, the peaks covered with fresh snow, and the bright virgin waters of the Rio Grande trickling from their multitude of secret beginnings under the rocks and the tundra and the alpine flowers. The elk were on the move, through the pines and aspen; in the evenings we'd hear the bull elk bugle forth his challenge to the world. That is another world, a sort of paradise compared to this, a world that these women and most of their children will never see.

Leaving the town behind, I drive for thirty miles northwestward along what is left of the river—the same sluggish green creek I saw at the shore of the Gulf—through cottonfields, citrus groves, and seedy plantation towns. Cotton and poverty, like coal and poverty, always go together. But the roads are lined with palms, and the old Rio Grande, unfenced and unguarded, meanders with tolerant indifference past poverty and wealth alike. The many horses in the lush pastures on either side of the river look content. Like the marsh hawks overhead and the dark green wild ebony trees in the fencerows, life in its various forms goes on, continues despite our human efforts to overcomplicate civilization and oversimplify nature.

Think about something pleasant. Think about the river, the Rio Bravo del Norte, as the Mexicans style it, the Great River, as writer Paul Horgan called it in his prizewinning book of the same name. The Rio Grande descends from the glorious mountains of Colorado and rolls into the high plains of New Mexico, carving a deep and narrow gorge through the black basaltic rock laid down over the eons by the old volcanoes of the region. Already diminished in volume and quality by irrigation farming upstream, the river nevertheless runs cold, clear, and deep enough to support a thriving population of native brown trout and hatchery rainbow trout, making it a favorite stream for Southwest anglers.

We camped here, too, for a couple of days, on the rim of the gorge a thousand feet above the river, near Taos. The water was low in mid-September. We could hear the murmur of the riffles, the cries of piñon jay and Clark's nutcracker. We saw a kingfisher and a mountain bluebird, flashes of color against the dark rock and olive drab sagebrush, and flocks of cliff swallows. A few local fly-fishermen stood on the gravelbars at the side of the river, near the dirt road and the antique structure known as John Dunn Bridge. Resolutely, over and over, they cast their lines; we saw no strikes.

On the other side of the river, the west side, some middle-aged flower children from the hip-boutique city of Taos were bathing in one of several natural hot springs at the river's edge. A few years earlier the native Chicano folk and the newly arrived Anglo hippies had been bitter enemies, but now, at the moment, things seemed peaceful enough. My wife and I cooked our supper over a fire of juniper coals and enjoyed the splendor of the evening.

Below Taos the Rio Grande emerges from its dark gorge and enters the broad valleys of north-central New Mexico. Here it passes some of the most colorful, picturesque, and richly historic towns and cities of the United States: Santa Fe, of course, most famous of them all; and then the ancient agrarian villages of the Pueblo Indians: San Gabriel, San Juan, Santa Clara, Puyé, San Ildefonso, Cochiti, Santo Domingo, San Felipe, Zia, Santa Ana, Sandia, and Isleta. Between San Ildefonso and Cochiti the river cuts into the mesas of the city of Los Alamos, home of the first atomic bomb and today, more than ever, an active center for nuclear research and weaponry. Intermingled with the Indian villages are the towns first settled by the Spanish some four hundred years ago—not only Taos, Albuquerque, and Santa Fe, but also Española, Algodones, Bernalillo, and many other little farming villages now gradually congealing into a continuous suburban mass from Albuquerque to the charming, handsome town of Socorro. Albuquerque is the major city of the state, a huge, dusty, windblown center of commerce and industry with a population, including its not-yet-annexed suburbs, of half a million souls, and growing daily.

Somehow in the midst of all this Spanish and Anglo-American pressure, the Pueblo Indians have managed to preserve a great deal, perhaps the best, of the outward forms of their centuries-old culture. But the agrarian and self-sufficient economy on which that culture was based, which formed the heart of its religion, ceremony, and customs, has been largely outmoded or absorbed. Its future seems problematic at best. When the children and grandchildren of corn farmers, deer hunters, and pastoralists study auto mechanics and computer programming, it seems unlikely that the roots and essence of an earth-based culture can survive.

But the river flows on, more or less, though drained of much of its volume by the countless development projects along the banks. At Albuquerque the Rio Grande is a broad, shallow stream, muddy gold, hemmed in by the enormous city on either side but still capable of sustaining cottonwood groves and a few farms along its shores.

South of Albuquerque, the Rio Grande enters the northern outreach of what geographers call the Chihuahuan Desert, a vast region of sand hills, gravel mesas, and isolated desert mountains. Here the juniper and piñon of the high range are seen no more; the typical plants are mesquite and the hardy creosote shrub, spreading from Socorro far south into Old Mexico. The dredged and diked river glides along through barren and largely uninhabited terrain, much like that of the Nile in southern Egypt.

Near the town of Truth or Consequences, New Mexico, the river is stoppered by Elephant Butte Dam, creating a forty-mile-long reservoir that is slowly filling up with silt and sediment washed down from the outlying drainage basins. From here to the Gulf of Mexico, the Rio Grande, like so many other American rivers, becomes more a canal than a river, dedicated completely to the needs of industrial agriculture and expanding municipalities. Cotton, alfalfa, pecans, peppers, and citrus serve a useful purpose for the ever-growing populations of the United States and Mexico, but the river itself, under such intensive management, offers little to other human needs—the need for natural beauty, for example, the need for physical and moral adventure.

With one great exception. About two hundred miles southeast of the city of El Paso, the Rio Grande, reinforced by its tributary the Rio Conchos from Mexico, has cut several magnificent canyons through the limestone plateau of Big Bend National Park. Two of them, Santa Elena Canyon and Mariscal Canyon, reach depths of more than fifteen hundred feet, with sheer vertical cliffs on either side; Boquillas Canyon is almost as deep.

Beyond Boquillas Canyon, at the eastern edge of the park, the river runs for another hundred miles through farther, if lesser, canyons, in a remote and largely roadless region inhabited only by a few cattle ranchers and a transient population of smugglers, illegal aliens, stray cattle, mountain lions, and wild horses. Friends and I have made several boat trips through these canyons, where the river alternates between stretches of lazy indolence and violent, white-water rapids worthy of respect. This is the most primitive country to be found along the Rio Grande, a harsh and lonely land of spectacular beauty.

Commercial raft trips are available in the upper canyons when the water flow is high enough, and Big Bend National Park is easily accessible to motorized tourism. Some of the best descriptions of the land and people of the Big Bend area can be found in Tom Lea's fine novel, *The Wonderful Country*, published thirty years ago but not forgotten.

At the old frontier town of Langtry, Texas, made famous a century ago by Judge Roy Bean, "the law west of the Pecos," the river leaves the desert mountains and begins its long, placid journey through the low hills and then the flatlands of southern Texas and northeastern Mexico. En route it bisects the twin cities of Laredo and Nuevo Laredo, roadhead of the Pan-American Highway, and one of the major gateways between the two nations.

For its final hundred miles, rapidly diminishing in volume, the Rio Grande again becomes the servant of humankind, nourishing another belt of cotton plantations, oilfields, citrus groves, and many towns and cities—Zapata, Falcon, Ciudad Mier, Roma, Los Saenz, Camargo, McAllen, Brownsville, Matamoros. Finally it twists and turns across a broad delta, no longer a river but only a little stream, to rejoin the source of all rivers, the open sea. There, under the power plant of the sun, the clouds are forming, day and night, to carry the precious water vapor back to the mountains once again, completing the circle.

A river, like truth, flows on forever and has no end.

So say the Chinese.

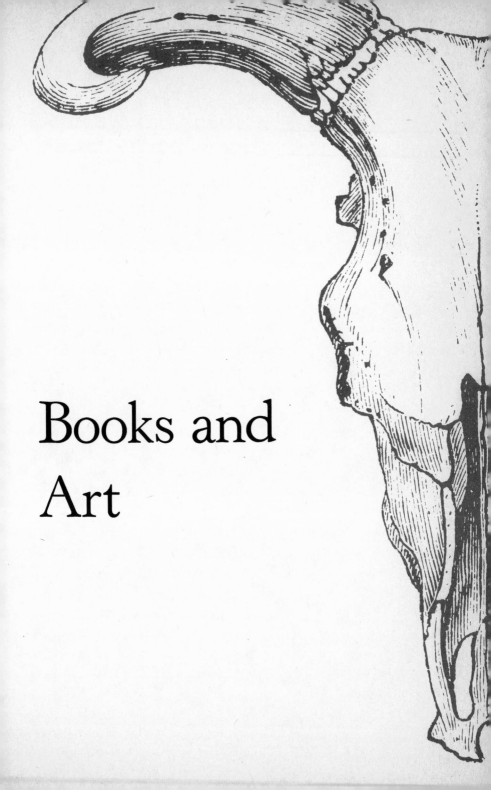

Books and
Art

A Writer's Credo

*I*t is my belief that the writer, the free-lance author, should be and must be a critic of the society in which he lives. It is easy enough, and always profitable, to rail away at national enemies beyond the sea, at foreign powers beyond our borders, and at those within our borders who question the prevailing order. Easy. And it pays. Ask the official guardians of Soviet literary morality. But the moral duty of the free writer is to begin his work at home: to be a critic of his own community, his own country, his own government, his own culture. The more freedom the writer possesses the greater the moral obligation to play the role of critic. If the writer is unwilling to fill this part then the writer should abandon pretense and find another line of work: become a shoe repairman, a brain surgeon, a janitor, a cowboy, a nuclear physicist, a bus driver. Whereof one fears to speak thereof one must be silent. Far better silence than the written word used to shore up the wrong, the false, the ugly, the evil. When necessary the writer must be willing to undertake the dangerous, and often ridiculous, and sometimes martyrlike role of hero or heroine.

That's all that I ask of the author. To be a hero, appoint himself a moral leader, wanted or not. I believe that words count, that writing matters, that poems, essays, and novels—in the long run—make a difference. If they do not, then in the words of my exemplar Aleksandr Solzhenitsyn, the writer's work is of no more importance than the barking of village dogs at night. The hack writer, the temporizer, the toady, and the sycophant, the journalistic courtier (and what is a courtier but a male courtesan?), all those in the word trade who simply go with the flow, who never oppose the rich and powerful, are no better in my view than Solzhenitsyn's village dogs. The dogs bark; the caravan moves on.

Why do I lay this special responsibility of speaking out upon the free-lance writer alone—notoriously a timid, reclusive, craven type? For several reasons. First, because the independent writer, his income derived from his readers and not from a newspaper chain or TV system or other industrial employer, has the freedom to speak the truth together with access—great or small—to some portion of the means of public communication. Freedom of speech means little to most citizens because for most there is no way by which they can reach more than a few of their fellow citizens. When TV, radio, newspapers, magazines are controlled by a few giant corporations, with editorial policies largely determined by the power of advertisers, then free speech—if not meaningless—becomes nearly powerless. In the United States we have thousands of newspapers, TV and radio stations, magazines and newsletters, but when nearly all say about the same thing on any issue almost all the time, what becomes of the value of the First Amendment to our Constitution? The guarantee of freedom of speech is one thing; the means and ability to exercise that right is another. Herein lies the function and the duty of those foolish enough to call themselves writers: to make full use of whatever means of free communication are available. The writer with an audience has that privilege, that power, that freedom—and therefore the moral responsibility to use it. Not to preach to his audience or to lecture them—who needs another sermon? another lecture?—but to speak *for* them, to let himself be used as the voice for those who share his view of earthly affairs, his emotions and discoveries, aspirations and hopes.

The writer, I'm saying, must be of use—must be useful to his people, to his community. Otherwise, who needs him? or her? If literary art, like so much of our poetry, music, and painting, is merely decorative, merely play and no more, then we can get by with wallpaper, polyurethane abstract sculpture, Bloomingdale's catalog, *Vanity Fair*, rock music (music to hammer out fenders by), and Andy Warhol. If literature, on the other hand, is to be more than Muzak, then it must be involved, responsible, committed (O dread clichés!). The independent writer is in a privileged position; therefore he works under special obligations. To do otherwise is to dishonor our profession.

Am I saying that the writer should be—I hesitate before the horror of it—*political?* Yes sir, I am. Yes ma'am, I am saying exactly that. And what do I mean by "political"? We'll get into it.

By "political" I mean involvement, responsibility, commitment: the writer's duty to speak the truth—especially unpopular truth. Especially truth that offends the powerful, the rich, the well-established, the traditional, the mythic, the sentimental. To attack, when the time makes it necessary, the sacred cows of his society. And I mean all sacred cows: whether those of the public-lands beef industry or the sacred cows of militarism, nationalism, religion, capitalism, socialism, conservatism, liberalism. To name but a few of our prevailing ideologies.

For instance: Motherhood. I am not alone in recognizing that the time has arrived (in view of the ongoing overpopulation catastrophe) to subject the idealization of Motherhood to a certain degree of intellectual pressure. But also its countercorrelative, Feminist Maternity: since motherhood really is a full-time, difficult, highly skilled, and essential human occupation (I speak from personal experience), women who do not wish to be mothers should not have babies. Or consider the interesting question of immigration, race, and culture: if we who still form the majority in America really care to preserve our democratic traditions, derived in the most part from our European heritage and ancestry, then we must be willing to reevaluate the possible effect of differential breeding rates and mass immigration from Latin American, African, and Asiatic countries upon those traditions. Touchy delicate explosive questions, I agree; even to mention them exposes the writer to abuse of the harshest kind. But the willingness to risk abuse for the sake of truth is one of the writer's obligatory chores.

He who sticks out his neck may get his head chopped off. Quite so. Nevertheless it remains the writer's moral duty to stick out the neck, whether he lives in a totalitarian state or in a relatively open society such as our own. Speak out: or take up a different trade.

Somebody has to do it. That somebody is the writer. If the independent author will not speak truth for us, who will? What will? Do we get truth from politicians? From the bureaucrats of big government? Or local government? Can we expect to hear truth from the U.S. Chamber of Commerce, the Teamster's Union, or United Technologies? Do we get much truth from *Time* or *Newsweek* or CBS or ABC or NBC or the daily press? From the TV evangelists of bunkshooter religion? Do we even get much truth from science and scientists? Well, as to that, we get some but not enough: most scientists are specialized technicians, each wedged into his niche of study, few of them capable of looking at life as a whole. Most scientists— in the East as in the West—sold their souls to industry, commerce, government, war, long ago. And what's the difference, anyway, among those massive and interlocking institutions? They form a monolith. A monolith in the shape of a pyramid. Whether laboring to launch our pharaohs safely into eternity or our astronauts into space, the fellaheen of the world have achieved little progress in modern times. By modern times I mean of course the last five thousand years. That trivial blip on the video screen of human history.

Since we cannot expect much truth from our institutions, we must expect it from our writers. Tolstoy said: "The hero of my work, in all of his naked unadorned glory, is truth . . ." Thoreau said: "The one great rule of composition is to speak the truth." And that other troublemaker said, "Ye shall hear the truth and the truth shall make ye free."

Truth, truth, what is truth? The word drops easily from the mouth but what does it mean? I venture to assert that truth for one thing is the enemy of Power, as Power is the enemy of truth. The writer, like the ancient Hebraic prophets, must dare to speak truth to Power and the powerful, face to face if need be. Hemingway said it once and said it good, in respect to Power: "A writer is like a gypsy. He owes no allegiance to any government. If he is a good writer he will never like any government he lives under. His hand should be against it and its hand will always be against him." (From a letter to Ivan Kashkin, his Russian translator, in 1935.)

What is truth? I don't know and I'm sorry I raised the point. I mean to dodge it if I can, for the question leads at once into a bog of epistemological problems too deep for me—or as I might say otherwise, beyond the scope of this essay. I will state only what I believe, that truth, like honor, generosity, tolerance, decency, is something real, that truly exists, whether we can define it or not. Subjectively, truth is that statement of cases which accords with my own view of the world—insofar as I have one—and which corresponds to the actual shape, color, substance of things and events—insofar as we can share and agree upon our perception of such matters. What is reality? For the purposes of daily life, as well as for the composition of stories, poems, and essays, I am willing to go by appearances. It appears to me, for example, that torture is wrong, a hideous wrong, and always wrong; that the death penalty—the cold-blooded infliction of death by instruments of the state—is an evil greater than murder; it seems to me, judging by appearances only, that it's wrong to allow children to die of malnutrition and equally wrong—worse than wrong, criminally stupid— to bring children into the world when you are not prepared to feed and care for them; it appears to me that the domination of many by a few, whatever the creed behind it, whatever the means, leads always to injustice and is therefore wrong, always wrong, leading to greater wrongs. I cite these banal, crude, and simple examples only to demonstrate that there is a moral area in which the true can easily be distinguished from the false. I cheerfully agree that there are other areas where the distinction is more difficult to ascertain.

But the writer's duty, I am arguing, goes beyond the utterance and support of commonly agreed-upon truths. Any hack can spout truisms, clichés, tautologies, and redundancies by the bookful. The task of the honest writer—the writer as potential hero—is to seek out, write down, and publish forth those truths which are *not* self-evident, not universally agreed upon, not allowed to determine public feeling and official policy. We can see this clearly enough when we look abroad. Most of us admire Solzhenitsyn for his courage in bringing to light the full extent and horror of the Gulag Archipelago and for defying his own government's effort to suppress his work. There are many other writers in the Soviet empire, less well-known than Solzhenitsyn, who continue to write and publish, through underground channels, the truth about what goes on in their native lands. There are similar writers at work, I hope, though we may not know their names, against the cruel and corrupt governments of South Africa, Kenya, Poland, Cuba, Chile, Zaire, South and North Korea, Ethiopia, Brazil, Indonesia, Vietnam, Guatemala, El Salvador and many other nations around the globe.

Easy enough to point out and condemn the faults and crimes of other nations. There's something relaxing in such exercises. But what about the writer's job in our own country, the US of A? To even mention the word *hero* in connection with the writer's lot in America invites laughter. The free-lance writer in this country enjoys so much freedom in his work, by contrast say with the dark plight of the writer in Central and Eastern Europe, that the American writer's chief concern is—and should be—to avoid making a fool of himself. The typical American writer has knowledge of very little but opinions on everything. Leaping at conclusions is his favorite calisthenic, snap judgments an intellectual reflex. The literary interview is a popular device through which the supercilious author provides facetious answers to superficial questions from skeptical reporters for the momentary entertainment of the bored and indifferent. In general the serious writer should avoid interviews and the serious reader should avoid reading them.

Nevertheless, I reassert with only slight modification my beginning announcement: the *American* writer, precisely because of his freedom, his unique position, his audience, his many and ample rewards, has the moral obligation to act as a critic of his own society, his own nation, his own civilization. Or abandon his pretensions.

Have I said or even hinted that social criticism is the writer's only duty? Or his primary duty? I have not. But it is, I repeat, one of his duties. And what should the critic criticize? What do we privileged Americans have to complain about?

But first: We have many critics of the critics, especially loud and dominant in this regressive, guilty, and servile decade. George Will, for example; William Buckley, for another; Tom Wolfe, for a third—and rising above mere columnar journalism, such distinguished literary gentlemen as Saul Bellow, John Updike, and the late John Gardner. To name but some. There are dozens of them. Hundreds. Their argument, compacted, amounts to this: communism has proved so gross an evil, the Soviet Union so dangerous an enemy, that by contrast America and its Allies appear as continents of light, exploding with human happiness. Therefore it is the writer's simple duty to condemn the former, praise the latter. Furthermore we exist in a state of ideological war with the powers of totalitarianism—the "present danger"— which makes it not merely heretical but treasonous to question our own government's policies, to doubt the glory of planetary capitalism, to object to the religion of endless economic growth, or to wonder about the ultimate purpose, value, and conse- quences of our techno-military-industrial empire. Those who persist in raising doubts and questions are attacked by defenders of order as the "adversary culture."

Very well: let us be adversaries. If the writer should be, among other things, a critic of his society, what does the Amer- ican writer, in this best of possible American worlds, have to complain about? Why the constant whining and carping by these literary pests who live in the richest, freest, happiest, *big* nation on earth? Who enjoy in addition the curious distinction of being paid, honored, even sometimes read, by inhabitants of the very nation-state which they seek, in their peculiar way, to sabotage, undermine, halt in its tracks, turn around?

Here I must speak for myself, acknowledging at the same

time that none of the opinions I presently hold on matters of state are in the least bit novel, original, or uncontroversial. Since they are, for the most part, banalities—but true banalities—I shall simply list them, not defend them.

1. The Soviet Union and the United States, while by no means morally equivalent, are basically similar in structure and purpose. Both societies are dedicated to nationalism, militarism, industrialism, technology, science, organized sport, and above all, to the religion of growth—of endless expansion in numbers, wealth, power, time, and space. In the SU, government controls industry; in the US, industry controls government; but each of the two great superstates is ruled in fact by an entrenched oligarchy—in the SU by the Communist Party; in the US by the power of concentrated wealth. (According to the Federal Reserve Board report of 1984, some 2 percent of US families control 40 percent of all assets.) We call our system a "representative democracy" but in fact our representatives, with honorable exceptions here and there, represent not the voters but those who finance their election campaigns. In the Soviet Union the egalitarian ideal of theoretical communism was betrayed from the beginning; in the United States the Jeffersonian vision of a decentralized society of independent agrarian freeholders was dead by the end of the nineteenth century while democracy, defined in Lincoln's words as "government *by* the people" has never even been tried.

2. Our century, the twentieth, has been a century of horrors. The century not only of Stalin's Gulag but of Hitler's concentration camps, where six million Jews, three million Russians, two million Poles, and half a million Gypsies were methodically put to death. But America has done its bit; last nation on earth

to abolish chattel slavery (and it required a civil war to accomplish that) we were the first to drop the nuclear bomb on our fellow humans, the Japanese—*after* their government had begun suing for peace. Then followed the thirty-year ordeal of Indochina (1945–1975), a great industrial undertaking whereby more millions of corpses were produced, an effort entirely financed and largely carried out by the American government. Our slaughters do not yet equal in magnitude those of Stalin and Hitler—but we tried, we are trying, and we're not finished yet. Meanwhile the threat of nuclear annihilation, succeeded by the nuclear winter, hangs over the entire planet, with the devices of destruction continually being developed, refined, and stockpiled on both sides. On several sides.

3. Old stuff. Consider a new idea, one that still seems absurd, even ridiculous, to most of the human population: I mean something called animal rights. The rights, that is, of the other animals (and plants) that share this still lovely, gracious, and bountiful world with us. I refer to the deliberate torture of monkeys, dogs, rats, rabbits, and other animals in the laboratories of what is called science, often for no purpose but the satisfaction of curiosity, the generation of unreadable monographs, and the development of commercial products such as cosmetics, patent medicines, and perfumes. I refer to the gruesome half-lives led by hundreds of millions of factory poultry, pigs, dairy cows, and feedlot cattle in our mass-production industrialized agriculture.

Perhaps my hero Solzhenitsyn would scorn my saying so but I am tempted to believe that the systematic cruelty inflicted upon animals trapped in our food and research apparatus is comparable—for who can measure the aggregates of pain, the sum of suffering?—to the agony that contemporary despotisms have exacted from human beings caught in their archipelagos of tyranny. Not merely comparable but analogous. Not merely analogous but causally connected. Contempt for animal life leads to contempt for human life.

4. I could easily go on all night, all week, with this bill of indictment. But shall note one crime more and call a halt. I mean the destruction, through industrialism, scientific technology, and multiplying human numbers, of the habitat of life. We are befouling and destroying our own home, we are committing a slow but accelerating race suicide and life murder—planetary biocide. Now *there* is a mighty theme for a mighty book but a challenge to which no modern novelist or poet has yet responded: Where is our Melville, our Milton, our Thomas Mann when we need him most?

Individuals do not live in isolation, nor do lovers, nor do families: any honest fiction or poetry which claims to deal with the lives of human beings must take into account the social context of those lives, directly or by implication. It's not a matter of restricting the writer to one mode of art—as in, say, the naturalism of Zola or the ponderous social realism of Dreiser—but rather of getting straight the connections between the fate of the author's fictional characters and the nature of the society which largely determines that fate. There is more truth in the sometimes airy fantasies of Kurt Vonnegut than in the tedious naturalism of John Updike's Rabbit Angstrom novels. Vonnegut writes as a critic of society; Updike in passive acceptance. As a result, assuming both do well what they set out to do, Vonnegut's work is more provocative, suggestive, meaningful—more interesting.

What I have said so far is much too crude, rough, plain, simple, even simple-minded to satisfy those who care about the arts of fiction, poetry, and essay. I recognize as well the banality of my basic argument, its old-fashioned overpolitical ring. Here I make the qualifications and reservations.

The author's primary task and the only thing that justifies his miserable existence is the writing of readable books worth reading: to have something interesting to say and to say it well. The writer's first job is to write, not aspire to a position of moral leadership. Quite so. Nevertheless—in and through the work, somehow, the writer must play his morally obligatory role as social critic, as spiritual guidon, as intellectual leader.

I present this plain and simple argument not to defend but to define an old and honorable tradition in American letters, one still alive despite temporary muffling by this gross, slimy, gluttonous slum of a decade, this Age of Reaganism and Servility. The majority of American writers today have chosen passive nonresistance to things as they are, producing sloughs of poetry about their personal angst and anomie, cascades of short stories and rivers of novels obsessed with the nuances of domestic relationships—suburban hanky-panky—chic boutique shopping-mall literary soap opera. When they do speak out on matters of controversy they attack not the evils of our time but fellow writers who may still insist on complaining. Updike, for example, in a recent review of Edmund Wilson's work, attacks Wilson for condemning the uses to which our federal government puts the money it extracts from American citizens. Wilson, in his grave for many years now, cannot respond to Updike's attack. But Wilson's words will live, I predict, long after Updike's fussy, prissy, precious novels have sunk into the oblivion they so richly deserve.

Edmund Wilson was the best of modern American literary critics. But good literary critics are plentiful, common as lichens on an academic wall; Wilson became a great American *writer* because he was more than a critic of books, he was a critic of the state, of society, of organized religion, of modern civilization. It is the grandeur of Wilson's vision that makes him a scandal to our literary courtiers queuing in the Rose Garden for their turn to kiss the First Lady's foot.

Here is Wilson in *Patriotic Gore* (1962), one of his best books. Try to imagine any prominent American author of the 1980s writing such words:

> We Americans, whose public officials keep telling us we live in the "Free World", . . . are expected to pay staggering taxes of which . . . 70 percent goes not only for nuclear weapons capable of depopulating whole countries but also for bacteriological and biological ones which make it possible for us to poison the enemy with every abominable disease from pneumonia and encephalitis to anthrax, cholera, diphtheria and typhoid. . . . If we refuse to contribute to these researches we can be fined and clapped into jail. . . . We are, furthermore, like the Russians, being spied upon by an extensive secret police, whose salaries we are required to pay, as we pay also the salaries of another corps of secret agents infiltrating foreign countries. And while all this expenditure is going on for the purpose of sustaining the United States as a more and more unpopular world power, as few funds as possible are supplied to educate and civilize the Americans themselves, who at worst live a life of gang warfare . . . in the buried slum streets of cities outside of which they can imagine no other world . . . while others find little spur to ambition when they emerge from four years in college to face two years in the armed services in preparation for further large-scale wars for which few feel the slightest enthusiasm.

Before Vietnam: imagine what Edmund Wilson would say were he alive today.

Wilson was never totally alone in his role as social critic. I have named Kurt Vonnegut, humanist and humorist in the Mark Twain tradition, whose work as a whole is alive with moral purpose. Remember the conclusion to his novel *Dead-Eye Dick*: "You want to know something? We are still living in the Dark Ages. The Dark Ages—they haven't ended yet."

There are others in the guard of honor, contemporary American authors whose books serve well as living in-print examples of what I am trying to say: Robert Coover, *The Public Burning*—a three-ring circus of a novel inspired by the trial and execution of the Rosenbergs; William Gaddis, *JR*—a maddening, hilarious, damning description of blind greed disguised as free enterprise; Thomas Pynchon, *Gravity's Rainbow*—a vast lament for humanity trapped in the engine room of our runaway technology; DeLillo, *Ratner's Star*—a satire on astrophysics, particle physics, and contemporary mathe-metaphysics. And Joseph Heller's *Something Happened*, the toughest analysis yet of the corporate mentality and the effect of such a mindset upon human life.

These are massive, complex, ambitious novels, elaborate efforts at taking a fix on the modern techno-industrial-military world. Difficult books, none were or ever will be very popular—but they prove that a concern with contemporary society combined with conscientious scrutiny through fiction results in works of high literary art, maximal not minimal. (The skies deluge us with cautious minimalists.) Their authors, if not heroes in the sense that Solzhenitsyn is a hero, were certainly heroic in the expenditure of effort, study, and thought that went into the making of such books. They serve my point: the writer worthy of his calling must be more than an entertainer: he must be a seer, a prophet, the defender of life, freedom, openness, and always—*always!*—a critic of society.

"Resist much, obey little," said Walt Whitman. What contemporary American poet writes words like those? Whitman also wrote, in the preface to the 1855 edition of *Leaves of Grass*:

This is what you shall do. Love the earth and the sun and the animals. Despise riches. Give alms to everyone that asks. Stand up for the stupid and crazy. Devote your income and labor to others, hate tyrants, have patience and indulgence toward the people, take off your hat to nothing known or unknown, or to any man or any number of men, go freely with powerful uneducated persons and the young and with the mothers of families. . . . Re-examine all you have been told at school or church or in any book and dismiss whatever insults your own soul. . . .

Radical talk in 1855; subversive and "naive" today.

Think of Mark Twain and *Huckleberry Finn*. Somewhere near the end of that greatest (so far) of American novels young Huck confronts a moral crisis: shall he or shall he not help return the runaway slave, Jim, to Jim's rightful owner? Huck knows, based on everything he has been taught by church and state, that he is committing an awful sin in helping Jim escape. Burdened by his acculturated conscience, he writes a message to Jim's owner, Miss Watson, giving away Jim's location. But hesitates in sending the message. Trying to decide what to do, Huck stares at the piece of paper that will betray his comrade Jim but save his own official soul:

It was a close place [thinks Huck]. I took it up and held it in my hand. I was a-trembling, because I'd got to decide forever betwixt two things, and I knowed it. I studied a minute, sort of holding my breath, and then says to myself:

"Alright then, I'll *go* to hell"—and tore it up. It was awful thoughts and awful words but they was said. And I let them stay said and never thought no more about reforming. I shoved the whole thing out of my head; and said I would take up wickedness again, which was in my line, being brung up to it, and the other warn't. And for a starter I would go to work and steal Jim out of slavery again; and if I could think up anything worse I would do that too; because as long as I was in, and in for good, I might as well go the whole hog. . . .

Exactly. Like Huckleberry Finn, the American writer must make the choice, sooner or later, between serving the powerful few or the disorganized many, the institutions of domination or the spontaneous, instinctive, natural drive for human liberation. The choice is not so easy as my loaded phrases make it seem: to serve the powerful leads to financial rewards, public approval and official honors, your picture on the cover of *Time* and *Newsweek* (or *Pravda* and *Izvestia*), and the eventual invitation to a White House (or Kremlin) dinner; to oppose the powerful creates difficulties, subjects you to abuse and scorn, leads often— as in the interesting case of Noam Chomsky, for example—to what we call the silent treatment in the literary press: your books are not reviewed; your views and reviews no longer appear in *The New York Times* or *The New York Review of Books*.

What is the author's proper role? How should the writer view his art? Speaking for myself now, perhaps only for myself, this is what I believe. This is what I tell the young. Call it one writer's credo:

Ignore the literary critics. Ignore the commercial hustlers. Disregard those best-selling paperbacks with embossed covers in the supermarkets and the supermarket bookstores. Waste no time applying for gifts and grants—when we want money from the rich we'll take it by force.

A literary career should be not a career but a passion. A life. Fueled in equal parts by anger and love. How feel one without the other? Each implies the other. A writer without passion is like a body without a soul. Or what would be even more grotesque, like a soul without a body.

There is a middle way between subserving the mass market and pandering to our Jamesian *castrati literati*. You do not have to write endless disquisitions about computer science professors seeking God while pursuing faculty wives. You do not have to write about male mutilation, lesbians in bearskins, Toyota dealers, or self-hating intellectuals longing for hierarchy, to work and live happily as a writer in America, God bless her such as she is.

You do not need to be analyzed, psychoanalyzed, Rolfed, e-s-t-ed, altered, gelded, neutered, spayed, fixed, acupunctured, Zenned, Yogied, New Aged, astrocharted, computerized, megatrended, androgynized, evangelized, converted or even, last and least, to be reborn. One life at a time, please.

What *is* both necessary and sufficient—for honest literary work—is to have faith in the evidence of your senses and in your common sense. To be true to your innate sense of justice. To be loyal to your family, your clan, your friends and—if you're lucky enough to have one—your community. (Let the nation-state go hang itself.) Among the Americans, read Walt Whitman, Mark Twain, Henry Thoreau, Theodore Dreiser, Jack London, B. Traven, Thomas Wolfe, John Steinbeck, Nelson Algren, and Dr. William Carlos Williams. For example. Emulate them until you find others emulating you. And then go on.

Why write? How justify this mad itch for scribbling? Speaking for myself, I write to entertain my friends and to exasperate our enemies. I write to record the truth of our time as best as I can see it. To investigate the comedy and tragedy of human relationships. To oppose, resist, and sabotage the contemporary drift toward a global technocratic police state, whatever its ideological coloration. I write to oppose injustice, to defy power, and to speak for the voiceless.

I write to make a difference. "It is always a writer's duty," said Samuel Johnson, "to make the world better." I write to give pleasure and promote aesthetic bliss. To honor life and to praise the divine beauty of the natural world. I write for the joy and exultation of writing itself. To tell my story.

Mr Krutch

*L*ike most people who knew him, I first met Joseph Wood Krutch in the pages of his books. During my student days I read *The Modern Temper* and was pleased by its austere pessimism. Then I read his studies of Poe, Samuel Johnson, and Thoreau and later, at approximately the same time that I was beginning to think about the subject myself, I read his justly popular books concerning the Southwest—*The Desert Year* and *The Voice of the Desert*. In the voice of Mr Krutch I found the clearest definition in contemporary literature of what many of us have felt, emotionally, intellectually, instinctively, to be the central meaning of the word *civilization*.

Civilization, if it means anything and if it is ever to exist, must mean a form of human society in which the primary values are openness, diversity, tolerance, personal liberty, reason. It appears doubtful that such a society has existed in the past and at present more doubtful that it will come to be in the near future—that is, within the next century or two. (Until some debris has been cleared away.) Nevertheless, civilization as here defined seems to me the one clear purpose implied in the martyrdom of prophets, the wisdom of seers and poets and thinkers, the suffering and torture of common people, that have characterized human history for the past five thousand years. If there is such a thing as human evolution (and I suspect there is) then the slow, painful effort toward a free community of men and women, with a full flowering of the individual personality, must be the ideal—always opposed but never wholly suppressed—which has inspired our long travail. If there is no such goal, then human history is indeed, as some have called it, nothing but a nightmare.

Among a thousand others one could name (Mann, Tolstoy, Kropotkin, Camus, Russell, William O. Douglas, Lewis Mumford, Aldous and Julian Huxley, for example), it seemed and still seems to me that Joseph Wood Krutch, in his modest but steadfast way, was one of the soldiers on the side of what we may properly term progress. Progress not as the politicians and technocrats have profaned the word, but progress in its larger sense, as the tortuous advance toward the idea of civilization. Mr Krutch's contribution to this campaign has been his communication of the discovery that the natural world must be treated as an equal partner. A world entirely conquered by technology, entirely dominated by industrial processes, entirely occupied by man and machine, would be a world unfit to live in. Perhaps impossible to live in. The technosphere of R. B. Fuller, the global village of McLuhan, the arcologium of Soleri, the noösphere of de Chardin, the planetary suburb of Herman Kahn, and suchlike visionaries (most of them already archaic), would be the ultimate trap for humankind, threatening us with the evolutionary dead end of the social insects—the formicary of the ants, the termite commune.

Mr Krutch did not deal, in his "nature" books, with these

global prospects, but confined his studies to the effects of the conflict in his own backyard, that is, the deserts of Arizona, Sonora, Baja California and the Grand Canyon of the Colorado. But as in any careful work, the results of regional investigations have planetary significance.

What I most admired in Krutch's work was not what he said—others said it too—but the way in which he said it. Many Americans and a few Europeans, influenced by the long Western tradition beginning with the heretical Saint Francis and carried on by Thoreau, were coming to share the same belief in the right of the nonhuman world to exist—to exist not only for the pleasure and health and instruction of humankind but for its own sake. Not only the pretty birds but also the predators and reptiles, the ugly and unloved, the organic and inorganic—all belong here with us, on the same small planet. In some sense of the word a boulder on a mountainside has a *right* to be left undisturbed, to *enjoy* its own metamorphoses in its own way at its own nonhuman pace of change. Mr Krutch came closer than any other contemporary American writer to supplying for such supposedly nonsensical notions the necessary supporting structure of rational thought.

Rational thought. Calm, reasonable, gentle persuasion. It was this quality of moderation in his writing that most impressed me, for my own inclinations always tended toward the opposite, toward the impatient, the radical, the violent. A book, I often thought, was best employed as a kind of paper club to beat people over the head with, to pound them into agreement or insensibility. Fully aware of my self-defeating tendencies as a propagandist, I suspected it would be both interesting and useful to meet Mr Krutch in person, face to face. Since we were both living in Tucson at the time I discovered his work, I soon found a pretext for paying him a visit.

The editor of an ephemeral magazine called *Sage* (referring not to sagacity but to a certain shrub popular in the American West) agreed to sponsor me as an interviewer of our most distinguished Southwestern author. I found Krutch's name and address listed in the telephone book and gave him a ring. Although he had never heard either of me or of *Sage*, he agreed readily to an interview. A few days later I knocked on his door. This was sometime in the winter of 1967–68; what follows is an account of the last formal interview that Krutch ever granted. At the time I did not know he was seriously ailing; he died not long afterward. Despite the triviality of my questions, our conversation may be of some interest to students and admirers of Krutch and his books.

Mr Krutch greeted me at the door, invited me in. He looked like a professor—thin, gray, a trifle abstracted. He looked older than I expected. We sat down in the scholar's traditional book-lined study.

As befitted his manner, appearance, and prose style, his speech was formal, almost pedantic. In other words he spoke in complete sentences and unified paragraphs, each thought leading logically into the next, like a man accustomed to lecturing. Or like a man accustomed to thinking. An odd sort of old bird. Tape recorder in motion, I began with the amateur interviewer's dumb initial question: "Mr Krutch, what do you think of interviews?"

He said he was willing to risk it. Having expected a much more lengthy reply, I found myself at a loss for the next question. Like many writers, I am a man of few words. Krutch meanwhile studied me gravely, waiting in silence, hands clasped on his stomach. I groped around for a while in the catacombs of my mind. (Have you ever been awakened from a good sleep by the sound of a crash somewhere deep inside the skull? That startling collapse, as of an eroded mudbank, when whole tiers and galleries of damaged brain cells give way and topple down the talus slopes of the cerebellum?) I ventured this:

"As a student of man and society, do you see much hope for our Southwestern cities? Tucson, for example?"

"A few years ago," he replied, after a pause, "I was dragooned into giving a speech at a luncheon of the Rotary Club here. The assigned subject was 'Tucson as a Place for the Writer' and I said that Tucson was still pretty good but getting less good every year. Whenever I see one of the billboards with the slogan 'Help Tucson Grow' I think, God forbid. And so I suggested to the Rotary Club that the slogan be changed to 'Keep Tucson Small.' They didn't follow my advice."

"Have you lived in other cities of the Southwest?"

"No, but I've seen them all."

"How do you like Las Vegas?"

"Las Vegas has a beautiful setting and the climate is very good. It might not be a bad place to live in. I don't suppose you have to see more of the Strip than you want to."

"Most people who do live there claim that, away from the Strip and Fremont Street, Las Vegas is much like any other American city."

"I suppose that's true, though I'm not sure that it should be considered complimentary. But the Strip for an occasional night is all right—if you like that kind of thing. You certainly won't find it held in such high esteem anywhere else."

"Have you been to the Grand Canyon lately?"

"I haven't been there in two or three years. Of course I got quite worked up about the threat of the dams. And I'm afraid that issue is not permanently disposed of yet. Many people here in Tucson, if they have connections with the business and political community, think it scandalous to oppose the dams. For example, the editor of the *Tucson Star* reviewed a new book of mine a couple of weeks ago. He praised the book highly for most of the review, then condemned it in his last few paragraphs because of my opposition to the proposed dams."

"I saw that review. I think he was mostly upset by your

criticism of hunting—hunting for sport, I mean. He seemed to think you were being unfair to sportsmen."

"I didn't know the piece would offend sportsmen. I was surprised by his indignation."

"Ever done any hunting yourself?"

"No. I hope I'm not fanatical on the subject but I don't like the idea of killing for fun."

"Haven't the sportsmen usually been good allies of the conservationists?"

"Not always. Now up in the Kaibab Forest the hunters wanted an open season on the Kaibab squirrel—a rare species. And they would have got it, too, if the Forest Service hadn't opposed them. The sportsmen will say, in the case of deer, that you've got to thin out the population anyway. And then I say, even so, I object to hunters doing it. Not so much for the sake of the deer as for the sake of the hunters. You see, I have this private, subjective feeling that killing things for the sake of sport is wrong. I think hunting is bad for hunters because killing for pleasure tends to brutalize those who do it. If it's a matter of thinning out excess populations, then by the hunter's logic we might as well start hunting each other."

Passing up my chance to defend sport hunting (I was once a sportsman myself—before I grew up), I suggested another topic: "Have you seen our newest national park—Canyonlands in Utah?"

"I've been on the edges of it."

"Have you heard about the proposals for the development of that park?"

"Only in a general way, but from what I've heard I hope they don't do it. On this question of development versus preservation, my belief is that some places should be open to maximum accessibility and others not. I think the idea that every national park should be developed in the same way is wrong."

"How about banning all cars from all parks?"

"I suppose I would approve of that idea, privately. Obviously it's not a practicable idea at present."

"Not politic?"

"Not politic. Too many people are accustomed to driving their cars through the parks. Take Yellowstone, for instance—we might as well let the auto tourists keep that one."

"A lost cause?"

"At present. But Canyonlands National Park is new, and as long as there are other easily accessible places in the area, like Arches National Park, with the same type of landscape, I can't see any need for new roads in Canyonlands. As I've said before, too many people use their automobiles not as a means to get to the parks but rather use the parks as a place to take their automobiles. What our national parks and forests really need are not more good roads but more bad roads."

"As a filtering device, you mean?"

"Exactly. There's nothing like a good bad dirt road to screen out the faintly interested and to invite in the genuinely interested. And it's perfectly fair and democratic, open to anyone willing to endure a little inconvenience and discomfort for the sake of getting away from the crowds."

Delving deeply, I managed to shovel up with mangled syntax a Serious Question: "Sir," I asked, "do you think there's any significant difference between man's relationship to the natural world in the desert and in other places, as in—well, say, New England?"

"I think that in both regions the opportunities to establish a relationship with the natural world are equally rich. And in both places there are many people who succeed in doing it. But I'm also afraid that in both there are too many people, as here in Tucson, who seem to be completely unaware of the existence of a natural world. I mean the men preoccupied with industry, property sales, merchandising—they're completely indifferent to anything that lies beyond commercial possibilities. At least they behave as if they are. But the Southwest is one of the few places where nature *invites*, or almost *demands*, human contemplation. And it is one of the few places in our country where contemplation of anything but walls and bars and other human bodies is still possible."

Pause.

"Whatever we think of our Southwestern cities," I said, "at least they're easy to get out of. Unlike back East, where the cities are merging into one another."

"True. One can drive a few miles from Tucson, turn off on a dirt road passable to an ordinary car, and spend hours in the desert without seeing another soul."

"Do you feel any need to justify this preference of yours for privacy? For solitude?"

"None whatsoever."

"Do you think the desert is in any way intrinsically more interesting than other regions?"

"I suppose it's primarily a matter of temperament. For myself, I like the openness of the desert, the barrenness of desert mountains. I was brought up in Tennessee and when I go back there and see those Appalachian mountains, beautiful though they are, I can't help feeling now that they're too heavily clothed in plant life; you can't see the basic forms. And also I suppose there's something dramatic about extremes—as in the desert and the jungle. In each, nature goes about as far as it can go in opposite directions. In one an extreme spareness, austerity; in the other an extreme of fecundity."

I said, "People used to regard the desert as ugly; now more and more seem to like it."

"Desert scenery appeals to modern taste—we now like spare, simple forms. Look at modern sculpture. And also, of course, the desert no longer seems dangerous. That makes a big difference. It must have been hard to appreciate the beauties of the desert when you were trying to get across it in a wagon train. In other words, for most people the wilderness does not become attractive until it is relatively safe. The eighteenth-century philosophers distinguished the 'awful' from the 'beautiful' by saying that the former suggested terror without being actually terrifying. Mountains, for instance, were 'horrid' until the eighteenth century made them merely 'awful.' Now that men are no longer terrified by mountains we call them 'beautiful.' "

"Have you any favorite books or favorite writers on the subject of the desert? On nature in general?" (I can't believe I said that. But it's on the tape.)

"From the standpoint of factual information I suppose Edmund Jaeger is as good as any on the Southwest. On the general subject of man's relation to the natural world I prefer the biologists who take what I call an out-of-doors attitude as opposed to the laboratory outlook. For example, Loren Eiseley, a beautiful writer, and the American naturalist Marston Bates."

"How about George Gaylord Simpson? Julian Huxley?" I had special reasons for mentioning these two writers. I was once seated next to Mr Huxley at a dinner. Since neither of us really wished to talk about evolution we found a mutual interest in discussing the latest mutations from London: Beatles and miniskirts. As for Dr Simpson, the famed paleontologist, author of *Horses* and other books, whom my friend the storyteller William Eastlake considers the only authentic genius he has ever met, he too was living in Tucson at this time. In company with Eastlake, I had recently spent an evening with Dr Simpson and his wife at their home. On that occasion, after some loose talk on my part about the Peace Corps, which I dismissed as "a typical piece of American cultural insolence," I had the distinction of hearing the great George Gaylord Simpson call me, to my face, the stupidest young man he had ever met outside of Harvard. (To Simpson, anyone under seventy was a young man.) I don't recall finding an answer to that remark; mainly, I was pleased with myself at having riled the authentic genius so easily. It was one of the high points of my life. As we were leaving Dr Simpson's house, rather shortly afterward, Eastlake informed me that Simpson's wife had been one of the prime organizers of President Kennedy's Peace Corps.

"Huxley and Simpson," Mr Krutch was saying, "come more under the heading of formal science than of nature writing, but they're both among the best in their fields."

This was interesting. I had asked Dr Simpson if he would like to meet Joseph Wood Krutch. He had said no. When I asked Mr Krutch if he would like to meet Dr Simpson, Mr Krutch said yes. Is this one of the key differences between the formal scientist and a mere literary type—the wider tolerance and greater curiosity on the part of the latter?

I said, "Isn't Simpson's approach to biology a great deal more mechanistic than yours?"

"Yes, but nevertheless he doesn't go the whole way. I'd much rather read him than a full mechanist. And Julian Huxley makes what I think is a responsible concession to my point of view, in that he allows at least some role to the idea of purpose in the evolutionary process."

"Have you a name for your style of humanism?"

"I've come around, I think, to a form of philosophical monism, so I suppose you could call me a monistic humanist. Or a humanistic monist. The terms don't mean much in themselves but they do mean that I am still not convinced that the universe is merely a machine, in the limited sense of that word. That is, I don't think it means anything to speak of 'materialism,' for example, because the potentialities of matter have just recently begun to be realized. When matter can be transformed into energy, we don't really know what the true nature of matter is."

"Or mind? Or consciousness?"

"That too. So that if one says that 'vitalism' is dead, as a theory in biology, he'd better add that 'mechanism' is also dead. It seems to me that the world is all one thing, not two. Mind and matter are not opposites but aspects of something underlying both. Matter becomes less and less material while mind is clearly one of the inherent potentialities of matter. But a lot of orthodox biologists are still unwilling to recognize this. They continue to think in nineteenth-century terms, assuming an absolute discontinuity between matter and consciousness, so that they're unable to explain how the latter can emerge from the former."

"There are some," I said, "who think the human mind is nothing but a miniaturized computer. Is that what you'd call laboratory thinking?"

"Yes. These are the same sort of technicians who used to compare the mind to a telephone system. But a telephone system never talks to itself. And neither does a computer. Some talk of the 'memory' of a computer, but there's no more justification for talking about the memory of a computer than the memory of a phonograph record. Both are mechanical means of bringing forth data or sounds previously placed there. Storage systems, not memories."

"Couldn't the human memory be considered simply a storage system?"

"The human memory is a creative storage system. No computer has yet been able to create anything."

This was getting too deep for me; time to change the subject. "Speaking of creation, are you working on a book now?" (Every writer's favorite question.)

"I'm not working on a book, except insofar as I am continuing to write magazine essays which someday may be collected in book form. For the kind of subject I'm writing about I probably get more readers in this way than I would in writing a book."

"Of your own books which do you like best?"

"I think the one called *Twelve Seasons* was the most deeply felt thing I've done. But an early one, *The Modern Temper*—which by the way, no longer suits my own temper—was the most popular of my books. No doubt because it was so pessimistic in outlook."

"Have you ever attempted to write a novel?"

"No. I'm afraid if I did, all my characters would tend to talk exactly like me. The nearest I've come to that sort of thing was in the imaginary dialogues between Johnson, Thoreau, and Shaw in my book *If You Don't Mind My Saying So.*"

"In which the characters quote from their own work."

"Yes. That way I made sure they wouldn't all sound like me."

"Are Thoreau and Samuel Johnson still among your intellectual heroes?"

"Oh yes."

"Aren't they nearly opposites, those two, intellectually and spiritually?"

"Yes, and like opposites they complement each other nicely. And they had this in common: both were uncompromising individualists."

"Do you keep up with current drama? Or with new fiction?"

"The last novelist I read with any great enthusiasm was Marcel Proust."

"What about James Joyce? Thomas Mann?"

"I've read both, and with interest. But neither quite suits me. I never could get through *Finnegans Wake*. Could you?"

"I've read the beginning and I've read the ending."

"Yes, I suppose that's the way most of us got through it."

"Do you still think Bernard Shaw will outlast them all?"

"Yes. I doubt if the others will be read a hundred years from now."

"How about some modern Americans—Hemingway? Faulkner?"

"Neither one of them have I read with any true satisfaction. In Hemingway I am repelled by that phony virility of his. I think it's a fake."

"He wrote good stories. Lots of good short stories."

"Oh yes. He really did have a gift for portraying character in a few words. When I read *A Moveable Feast* I was struck by the accuracy of his perceptions. I knew some of the people Hemingway writes about in that book and even if he had not named them I would have recognized them easily, simply from his brief descriptions."

"Perhaps Hemingway was better at seeing the truth in others than—"

"Than in himself—that may be."

"And Faulkner?"

"I can't get through the jungle of his sentences."

"Because you're a desert lover."

"That might be the trouble."

I sensed that the good Mr Krutch was getting bored with me. Or tired. Couldn't blame him. I proceeded to wrap the thing up quickly. "You've written much on literature and drama, on other writers, on nature, on modern society, on contemporary science and thought. What would you say your chief interest is these days?"

"I'm still very much interested in nature and the spectacle of nature. But I suppose most of what I've been writing recently tends to center around the question of the reality of consciousness as opposed to a strictly mechanistic view of life. And around the opposition between traditional human values and the new technology . . ."

End of the tape. Mr Krutch invited me to stay for lunch. I met his wife, Marcelle, a wise and witty woman; we talked of other things, including the Vietnam War. I was unable to get him to take a stand against what seemed to me then and seems to me now the most shameful episode in our nation's history since the time of legalized human slavery. Krutch, in early 1968, could not yet bring himself to believe ill of President Johnson, whom he much admired for his achievements in civil rights. Perhaps later he changed his mind; I don't know. He didn't have much time left. I never saw him again.

In his "nature" books, Krutch explores in detail many of the themes mentioned in my depthless interview. He takes an over-all view, beginning with protozoa and ending with the human— and with the song of a cardinal outside his window, finding in the latter the suggestion that joy, not the struggle for survival alone, is the essence of life, both its origin and its object. One may quibble with some of his objections to Darwinian theory— the elegance of the idea of natural selection, for example, lies in the fact that it still appears, after a century and a half of scrutiny and attack, to serve as *sufficient* explanation for the method of evolution—without denying Krutch's thesis that there is far more in the character of living things, human and oth-erwise, than can be understood through statistical analysis, chemical reaction, or any kind of quantitative measurement, however refined. In his unwavering insistence, to the very end of his life, on the primacy of freedom, purpose, will, play, and joy, and on the kinship of the human with all forms of life, he defended those values which supply the *élan vital* of human history.

Joseph Wood Krutch was a humanist, one of the last of that endangered species. He believed in and he practiced the life of reason. He never submitted to any of the fads or ideologies or fanaticisms of the twentieth century. In his last completed book, *And Even If You Do* (following logically upon *If You Don't Mind My Saying So*), he quotes from a letter written by Marguerite Yourcenar, the historical novelist, to a friend:

> I tell myself that you are lucky to have lived during an epoch when the idea of pleasure was still a civilizing idea (which today it no longer is). I am especially pleased that you have escaped the grip of the intellectuals of this century; that you have not been psychoanalyzed, and that you are not an existentialist nor occupied with motiveless acts; that you have on the contrary continued to accept the evidence of your understanding, your senses, and your common sense.

Madame Yourcenar's testimonial will serve as an apt description of the character of Joseph Wood Krutch himself. In this age of the myopic specialist and the cosmic expert, of the crazy, the extreme, and the violent, I can think of few higher tributes to offer to his memory.

The Remington Studio

At the heart of any paint-
er's life must be his studio, his place of work. For one great
painter of the American West, Frederic Remington (1859–1907),
that place was a large and airy room in his home near Long
Island Sound in New Rochelle, New York.

New York? Quite so: like most of the famous artists of the
West—Moran, Bierstadt, Catlin, Bodmer, Miller—Remington
too was an Easterner, a born-and-bred New Yorker. Like the
others, Remington hunted and gathered his material, found his
themes and took his subjects from his many travels through the
West in the late nineteenth century. He made thousands of
sketches in the field—out there in the sunburnt deserts, among
the vivid hills and mountains, on the buffalo-haunted plains—
but created the illustrations, paintings, and sculptures that made
his fortune and fame in the studio at his home in New Rochelle.

Remington came under the influence of the French Impres-
sionists late in his career, after the turn of the century, and his
final paintings reveal an increasingly deeper absorption in tone,

light, color, form—the "painterly qualities" that Van Gogh, Cézanne, and Gaugin made primary. But despite this later emphasis on surface rather than detail and content, Remington was always a believer in the truth of fact, the poetry of the actual. All of his work, early and late, displays his fidelity to the truth of what he saw. Like most conscientious craftsmen, he did not rely solely on memory and imagination but reinforced both with the reality of tangible, material *things*. His guarantee of authenticity lay in the artifacts that he carried home with him from his Western expeditions, a treasure and treasury of mostly handmade objects that were in themselves both practical tools of their trade for the men who used them and works of art in the eyes of a man like Frederic Remington. "No ideas but in things," wrote our all-American poet William Carlos Williams. Remington seems to have anticipated that statement; his New Rochelle studio was liberally furnished with a visual feast of durable objects that seem to grow richer in value the longer they survive in time.

Remington died seventy-nine years ago. His art survives, as popular now as it was during his lifetime. The interior of his marvelous studio has also been preserved—no longer in New Rochelle, New York, but in the appropriate setting of the Whitney Gallery of Western Art, a part of the Buffalo Bill Historical Center in Cody, Wyoming. Through the labor of his admirers (and generous donations of money) the place of Remington's work has been reconstructed in precise detail, refurnished, and restored intact to the region that was always his source of inspiration.

One cannot imagine a better place for a Remington museum than the small town of Cody. To the northeast and east lies an open plain: formerly buffalo country and a hunting ground for various tribes of nomadic horse-culture Indians, later to become prime cattle range, as it still is, a land of ranchers and cowboys.

For fifty miles to the southeast, before and beyond the Greybull River, is a landscape of badlands, soft hills of blue clay resembling melted elephants, purple cliffs, auburn buttes, red pinnacles of bentonite and mudstone—a painted desert empty of human habitation and nearly waterless. South and southwest of Cody stand the mountains in wave after wave: the twelve-thousand-foot crags of the Carters and Absarokas and the jagged snow-covered peaks of the more distant Wind River Range. West of Cody is the gateway to Yellowstone, where the seething silt-brown snowmelt of the Shoshone River races downward through the dark gorge called Shoshone Canyon.

Cody is a tourist town—how could a place founded by Colonel William F. Cody, a Buffalo Bill center, be anything else? Even without the name, the region surrounding the town seems to exhibit in one grand sweep every major feature that, taken together, the American West is supposed to offer. It's not *all* here but there's more than enough to satisfy. Quite fitting then that the Whitney Gallery should have been built here in 1959; and that in 1981 the replica of the Remington Studio was added to it.

On a rare afternoon in June the hard-edged cumulus clouds drift across the hot violet of a Wyoming sky. The great mountains with their snowy summits shimmer beyond a scrim of heatwaves. The avant-garde of the summer's tourist traffic streams through town without stopping, bound for Shoshone Canyon, the forty-mile-long Wapiti Valley, and Yellowstone National Park. Some of us leave the highway, though, on the west end of Cody, for a visit to the Historical Center, a spacious and handsome modern building enclosed in cool green gardens of grass and poplars. We park our metallic steeds beneath the equestrian bronze statue of *The Scout*, Cody himself, mounted on a plinth of pink native granite. (Fine word, plinth.) Inside the building we turn to the north wing, enter the Whitney

Gallery, and find the alcove reserved for Frederic Remington.

Many of his oils hang on the alcove walls but the immediate attraction here is the reconstructed studio with its display of Western Americana. The room is illuminated by north light from a sloping skylight twelve to fifteen feet above the floor and from a smaller window in the wall. A brick fireplace with black andirons dominates the room; the antlered head of a bull moose above the mantel gives the room the rustic sporting air of a hunting lodge. Antique handguns and rifles, crossed cavalry sabers, and Plains Indian warclubs hang on the walls, together with such domestic articles of frontier life as a brass canteen, wooden snowshoes with rawhide lacings, braided quirts and bridles, chaps, buckskin leggings, a variety of broad-brimmed Mexican hats, a homemade fiddle with bow, powder horns, leather pipe bags, doeskin shirts decorated with Sioux bead-work, Indian blankets, buffalo horns, braided lariats, a fully beaded Cheyenne cradle board, a pipe tomahawk, Indian masks and drums, a rattle made from a turtle shell, a Sioux warrior's buckskin shield. These are some of the *things themselves* which supplied the precise detail Remington wanted in his illustrations.

On the fireplace mantel are skulls—human, animal—and dangling from it six ceramic drinking mugs. On the floor are saddle stands with old Indian and cavalry saddles, a pair of Army-style riding boots stuffed with shoe trees, pots and kettles of copper, Indian baskets, trunks, chests, a table with palette and brushes, a light easel in one corner and a massive large dark-stained easel near the center of the studio. On each easel rests an unframed, unsigned oil painting—work left not quite complete at the artist's death. In front of the fireplace, on an Indian rug, is a comfortable wooden chair and beside it a coffee cup in a saucer and a few pieces of unopened mail addressed to Frederic Remington.

The painting on the smaller easel depicts two Indian women, dressed in nineteenth-century buckskin, planting seed in the midst of a featureless prairie. The painting on the big easel shows a sagebrush draw leading up between tawny hills toward snow-streaked mountains in the background. One a scene from the past, the other a scene from what could be the present, both evoke with subtle and economic skill a deep, full, haunting sense of the American West as it really was and as it really is today. The artist in his studio, three thousand miles away, transcends through the magic of his art the gulf of space and time between New Rochelle, New York, and Buffalo Bill's Cody, Wyoming—between then and now—between the wonder that was and the beauty that yet remains.

The Future of Sex

A Reaction to a Pair of Books—
Susan Brownmiller's Femininity *and*
Gloria Steinem's Outrageous Acts

What is femininity? Like the beautiful in art and nature, femininity in woman is one of those qualities we think we recognize instantly, whether or not we are able to provide a rational definition. Like most men, I suppose, the first thing I sense in approaching another member of the human race is the sex of that person. Another male? Or a *female*? (*Emphasis* added.) If another male, my reaction is one of indifference, unless the circumstances are such as to suggest an element of danger in the situation. But, if it's a female, a little flag goes up, automatically, somewhere in the nervous system—and we humans have extremely nervous systems—and that little flag stays up, waving, until closer inspection enables me to determine the most important consideration: namely, Is she sexually attractive? If yes, the flag stays up for as long as that female is present in my consciousness. If no, the flag droops immediately, furling itself about my pendant pole in a state, again, of relative indifference. No matter if the woman's name is Margaret Thatcher or Margaret Truman or Margaret of Angoulême—my head may be willing to pay her polite attention, but the vital spark of erotic electricity is absent, seeking elsewhere for its magnetic polarity.

Now this is a hell of a way to react to my fellow man. But there it is, an involuntary reaction no more under my direct control than the beating of my heart or the breathing of my lungs. Unless I were to become a Yogi ascetic of some exotic and esoteric kind, the matter is out of my hands. Such is the nature of the male primate. From his point of view, all females are divided at once, emphatically and radically, into two distinct classes: those he desires and those he can ignore. Could there ever be a nicer, neater definition of the male sexist pig? And what makes that difference between the two classes of females? Nothing less than the completion of the circle: *femininity*, our pretty word for female sexual attractiveness, the subject of Brownmiller's book and the bane of Steinem's long campaign for equality and a full share in power.

In her deeply interesting and touchingly even-tempered essay, Brownmiller probes this always intriguing subject in fascinating detail—fascinating to me, at least, as it should be to most men, but perhaps tiresome and all too familiar to women. The essence of the fascination lies in the traditional male conviction (which I share) that women, while apparently members of the same species, are creatures so fundamentally different from men, so much our moral, aesthetic, and spiritual superiors as to seem to us like beings of a different race, from a different world, inhabiting a separate sphere. And of course we men like it that way; it is the difference, not the similarity, which creates the tension and the delight. It is a neverending source of wonder to us that we are even able to interbreed with them—and that they permit it—even encourage it, through that delicious variety of form and dress, arts and graces, that both sexes—the various sexes—call "femininity."

Brownmiller divides her analysis of femininity into seven parts: body, hair, clothes, voice ("Her voice was low and soft / A comely thing in woman"), skin, movement, and emotion. With good humor superimposed on an underlying sense of resentment, she describes the thousand and one devices by which, from girlhood on, the female of the species endeavors to make herself more interesting to men. It's all here, the stuff of *Seventeen* and *Glamour* and *Cosmopolitan*, the woman's endless struggle to achieve and then preserve what we call a "shapely" figure; glossy and flowing hair (preferably blond); clothing that combines the virtues of modesty and decorum with an essential flirty, eye-catching sexual provocation; a manner of speaking that suggests both vulnerability and compliance; the necessary clear, rosy, healthy skin; a style of bodily motion emphasizing suppleness and sensuality; and the emotional freedom, openness, liberality, that connotes responsiveness to and sympathy for others—as opposed to the stern self-absorption of the aggressive, hard-driving, ambitious man. These are the very qualities men love in women—and that the programmatic contemporary feminist most detests.

We're familiar with the basic thesis. "Femininity," argues Brownmiller, is not so much a reflection of biological differences as it is a cultural imposition, a set of inhibiting rules that forces women into a permanent secondary role in human affairs, making them a subject class, the subordinate sex, unable within such constraints to compete on a fair and equal basis with men.

Are not men bound within a matching system of rules, equally desirous of attracting women? Yes and no, says Brownmiller; men desire women but their means for winning the favor of women are different, based not on physical allure but on the show of power—bodily strength in traditional societies, and money, status, influence, and prestige in techno-industrial societies. These attributes result from the successful pursuit of power, conferred by reflected light upon women who succeed in winning the affection and thus the support of stronger men, a woman's best hope for social security. Diamonds remain a girl's best friend—diamonds, Cadillacs, a big important house in the suburbs, and an alimonial lock on a powerful man's income.

Why should women agree to play this miserable game? They must, says Brownmiller, because society's rules are such that most women cannot themselves achieve the status, power, and prestige they envy in men. And one of the rules that keeps them down is the rule of femininity. We seem to be trapped in a vicious circle that prevents women—and men too—from attaining their full potential as human beings. Indeed we are, says Brownmiller, and so it is. But she offers no clear-cut solutions, merely the unwritten hint that women should strive to become more like men and men more like women. Androgyny. The future, if we have one, belongs to the androgynes. She implies here and there in her book that she has misgivings about such a resolution of the great sexual war, but the logic is clear.

Gloria Steinem suffers from no such reservations. In her collection of journalistic essays, written over a period of twenty years, she makes perfectly plain what her goals are: full equality through an equal sharing of political, economic, and sexual power. Her message is "subversive," she claims, and her aim "revolutionary." "Some women and men," she concedes, "seem to need each other," but that mutual need should not lead to dependency on the part of women or domination on the part of men. Be like me, implies Steinem: Deny the need.

What a strange tangle of hope and anger. "*Some* women and men *seem* to need each other." That in itself is a baffling statement. If nearly all men and women did not absolutely *require* each other the human race would never have survived, much less emerged from the jungles and savannahs of Africa. (The

Aborigines of Australia believe that humankind was delivered from a crack in Ayer's Rock, a womb-shaped monolith near Alice Springs. Not an unreasonable theory either.)

Steinem's revolutionary rhetoric boils down to mild reformism, a program of four main parts. Number one: equal pay for "comparable" work. Why not, if anyone can figure out a formula for defining "comparable" work. Number two: reproductive freedom—by which she means the freedom *not* to reproduce, the right to contraception and abortion on demand. Most of us grant the fairness of that; no woman should be compelled to bear a child against her will; compulsory maternity amounts to rape by the state. Number three: an equal sharing of political power. I am not much impressed by Indira Gandhi or Margaret Thatcher, but if some women want political power, and the economic power that goes with it, let them seek it and take it. The means are available; women form a majority of the voting population in America and most other Western nations. Number four: "cultural parity." Here's the sticky one, by which Steinem means not only the right of women to pursue careers but also, for those peculiar men and women who seem to need each other and who wish to participate in the mainstream of life by creating children and forming families, the "persuading or forcing" of men to perform half the routine household chores traditionally assigned to their wives, including a fifty-percent share in the duties of what is now called "parenting." (I've seen mothers. I've seen fathers. I don't think I've ever seen a "parent.") You might think this a private matter best left to each couple to work out on a basis of mutual agreement; any rigid pattern imposed by feminist doctrine can only lead to intrafamily conflict to be settled in the modern American way, that is, by divorce. Some men can accept the job of househusband, and normal men have strong paternal instincts. But to expect the majority of men to care for children exactly as mothers do, abandoning the million-year-old male urge to range beyond the nest in search of adventure in the company of other men, is to expect too much—is asking for trouble. The fact that our industrial civilization makes man's traditional role highly difficult to fulfill is the major source of male unhappiness and the primary cause of domestic strife and marital breakup. But this is the world men have created. Again we see that the future lies with androgyny.

For how can women compete with men, share power with men, become the full equals of men, without becoming much like men? Facing this distasteful prospect, the feminists demand that men meet women halfway. In other words men should neuter, geld, caponize themselves by becoming as much like women as possible, reducing sexual differences to mere anatomical appendages, trivializing sex itself to another form of play, a harmless game, unisex recreation, inconsequential fun. A world of androgynes, encapsulated in beehive cities, fiddling with buttons penile, electronic, and clitoral—that is the future beloved alike by the technocratic futurologists and the thoroughly logical radical feminists. Cut off from their primordial animal natures, denying the biological wellspring of life, reproducing themselves through the artificial insemination of laboratory wombs, the inhabitants of this glittering metallic city will live to the full the existence of rationally programmed robots. And what is the ideal robot but a properly processed human being?

Both Brownmiller and Steinem would dismiss my prognosis as juvenile fantasy. Steinem's "revolution" is illustrated by her favorite example, the "ring-around-the-collar" controversy. It is not enough, she says on her lecture tours, for the woman to ask that her man wash his neck; that is mere liberal reformism. No, she says, demand that the rascal *wash his own shirt*. And she concludes her revolutionary appeal by urging women to support Walter Mondale for president—and by condemning babies and little children to federally funded day-care centers while their mothers fulfill their human potential in offices, boutiques, boardrooms, army tanks, or coal mines. *Outrageous*.

"In the world we live in," wrote Doris Lessing, "feminism is a trivial cause." The woman's movement, Joan Didion says, "is no longer a cause but a symptom." "Each sex should do the kind of work it is best suited for," wrote Margaret Mead, "although no one should be barred from any work *because* of sex."

Mired in confusion in a confused society, feminism today seems cursed by triviality—the latest form of woman's ancient curse. But I suspect that both the movement's evangelists and its critics may be wrong. There *is* a revolutionary potency in feminism because the apparent future, the general drift of technological society, is toward that androgynous world I have sketched above, a world where unisexual, interchangeable, replaceable units of desexed semihumanity carry on the subjugation of nature and human nature in a universe dominated by interlocking, embracing, copulating machines.

I hope that we are all wrong. I hope that somewhere on the far fringes of the future, deep in the surviving jungles, high in the isolated mountains, far out in the forgotten deserts, little bands of free men and liberated women may still be roaming, hunting, fishing, gathering, begetting and mothering human children, awaiting their opportunity to attack the corrupt cities, to sack the temples of technology, to ravish and raze (once again!) the leaning towers of babble.

Yes—and then what? To simply repeat the whole wearisome cycle one more time? Or to find another way, a better way? A truly human way?

I wish I knew. We are dreamers, every one of us. I console myself with a single fierce resolve—the drama must go on. Women and men share not only their beds, their food, their homes, their lives, but also a common fate. The continuity is all.

Emerson

Where He Came From

Ralph Waldo Emerson— first American author of distinction, a poet, lecturer, amateur philosopher and theologian, leader of that school of thought (and feeling) known as New England Transcendentalism. Born in Boston—where else?—his father a Unitarian minister of local fame who died in 1811, Ralph Waldo and his five siblings were raised by a pious mother and a well-educated aunt from the father's side of the family.

Emerson attended the Boston Latin School (a sort of prep school) from 1813 to 1817, where he acquired the traditional rudiments of a classical education. He then spent four years at Harvard, graduating without distinction or honors, apparently only a mediocre student. He supported himself as a schoolmaster while continuing his studies at the Harvard Divinity School. "My reasoning faculty is weak," he confesses in his *Journal* in 1824 ·(aged twenty-one), explaining to himself his decision to become a clergyman. "But," he goes on, "the preaching most in vogue at the present day depends chiefly on the *imagination* [italics added] for its success, and asks those accomplishments which I believe are most within my grasp." A shrewd self-analysis—and it marks the stage in Emerson's life when he began to understand himself well and to gain an understanding or premonition of his future role as a literary artist. Emerson, more than anything else, was a writer, a scrivener of the imagination. (Thus Nietzsche, who was much influenced by Emerson, admiring his "manifoldness" and "cheerfulness," recognized Emerson as one of the nineteenth century's masters of prose.)

How He Got That Way

As we would expect, the doctrines of Unitarian Christianity were the first major influence on Emerson. But they were not the most extensive or long-lasting. The sort of preaching that Emerson would excel at (and he certainly was a preacher) has little to do with any established church or even with Christianity in general.

In the winter of 1826–27 Emerson took a trip to Florida for reasons of health and there happened to meet and talk with a French writer named Achille Murat, whose "consistent Atheism" was combined, to Emerson's surprise, with a high concern for moral issues. Young Emerson never dallied with atheism, as such, but his brief encounter with the impressive, aristocratic Murat certainly knocked down a few walls in Emerson's developing mind and led him into even more exotic realms.

By the late 1820s our young theologian had read a prodigious amount of philosophical and occult books, including writings by Zoroaster, Confucius, Muhammad, Plotinus and other neo-Platonists, Leibniz, Rousseau, Edmund Burke, Hume, von

Herder and, perhaps most important, the eighteenth-century mystic and visionary Emmanuel Swedenborg, whose neo-Platonic notions of a "world soul" and "correspondence" would reappear, somewhat transformed, in the essays of Emerson.

Emerson was also much influenced by the new cultural movements in Germany, especially advanced biblical criticism which was undermining traditional Christian theology, and the philosophical idealism of Hegel and Fichte, as these were taken up and interpreted for the English-speaking world by the literary Romantics Coleridge, Wordsworth, and Thomas Carlyle. It was from Coleridge's *Aids to Reflection* (1825) that Emerson derived his pseudo-Kantian distinction between "Reason" (meaning intuition of truth) and "Understanding" (meaning the empirical observation of material facts)—roughly speaking.

Meanwhile his physical, worldly life continued. In 1829 Emerson became pastor of the Second Church of Boston; in 1830 he married Ellen Tucker; in 1831 his young wife died of tuberculosis, a popular disease in the nineteenth century. (Thoreau too would catch it.) Her death had an anguishing yet liberating effect on Emerson: he questioned himself about immortality and preached sermons that expounded early versions of his ideas on "self-reverence" or "self-reliance" and "compensation" (for every loss an equal and compensating gain). Absorbed in his intellectual adventures, he became bored with weekday Bible classes and in 1832 resigned his position at the church. Early the next year he took ship to Europe, determined to meet in person, face to face, the writers whose words had so excited his mind.

In this he only partly succeeded. During his short stay in England he met and talked briefly with Wordsworth, Coleridge, and Carlyle, becoming a lifelong friend of the third. This first of his three European tours was important in shaping Emerson's basic philosophic outlook, as poetically expressed in his major essays soon afterward. His unsatisfactory conversations with these famous men had chiefly the effect of convincing young Emerson (he was now twenty-nine) that his best guide to solving the problem of life's meaning was his own intuitive insight into himself. As he put it, "There is really nothing external; like a spider I must spin my thread from my own bowels." He decided that "the purpose of life seems to be to acquaint a man with himself" and that "the highest revelation is that God is in every man."

On the ship back to America in September of 1833 he wrote in his *Journal*, "There is a correspondence between the human soul and everything that exists in the world." He also wrote, "Since a man contains all that is needful to his self-government within himself, it follows that nothing can be given to him or taken away from him but always there is a compensation." Correspondence and compensation: two of the key notions that Emerson would endeavor to elaborate for much of the rest of his life, first in his original Transcendentalist manifesto *Nature* (1836), and then in most of his later works, including *Essays* (1841 and 1844), *The Conduct of Life* (1860), and *Society and Solitude* (1870).

In 1835 Emerson married again, this time to Lydia Jackson, with whom he had several children and apparently enjoyed a tolerably serene and comfortable domestic life. Leaving Boston for good, the Emersons moved in with Emerson's mother in her large and handsome house in nearby Concord. There Emerson lived most of the rest of his life, except for his frequent and extensive lecture tours across America and in Europe. In Concord Emerson's writings, his friendships with people like Thoreau, Hawthorne, and Margaret Fuller, his appealing and sagelike personality, his editorship of the magazine *Dial* and his leadership of the Transcendentalist movement earned him a reputation as a national and then international man of letters—the best-known and most admired writer in America in his time.

The Man and His Notions

Emerson was not a professional philosopher. His vague and cloudy ideas regarding "correspondence" and "compensation," "self-reliance" and the "Over-Soul," "Reason" versus "Understanding," "Polarity" and "Pre-established Harmony" were never meant to bear serious philosophical scrutiny. To regard Emerson as a philosopher would be to miss the peculiar significance and merit of his work. He was not a metaphysician but an intuitive wise man and poet. "In Emerson," wrote his early admirer Nietzsche, "we have *lost* a philosopher."

Like his artistic models Montaigne, Pascal, and Goethe, Emerson was a virtuoso of the well-phrased thought in which style and idea, symbol and meaning, are inseparable. His meditations are exploratory rather than technical and definitive; he attempts to enrapture and ensnare the reader through the use of language as revelation rather than as proposition and logical argument. The enjoyment of Emerson's writing is more a matter of literary criticism than of philosophical analysis. Emerson's method was the assembly of a literary mosaic, the accumulation of epigrams and aphorisms on a single broad theme, such as nature, friendship, immortality, usually in the form of an essay, lecture, or formal address. Son of a preacher, trained as a preacher, Emerson writes in homiletic fashion: his works are secular sermons that differ from the sermons of his ancestors, the Puritan divines, chiefly by virtue of a greater breadth and subtlety of message, and by the intense personalism of his inner soliloquy: in Emerson we hear a man thinking to himself—but thinking aloud and doing it over the length of a long and (in words) very productive life. (The collected works comprise twelve fat volumes.)

Emerson remains interesting to us, a century after his death, because he was one of the first American writers to deal wholeheartedly with the ideological perplexities of his time, when the ancient Christian faith had seemingly broken down while no satisfactory new ideology had arisen to replace it. The nineteenth century was (for the literary set) an age without faith but, as Carlyle said, "terrified by skepticism." (In this it resembles our own time and is indeed the prologue to it.) Emerson tried to discover for himself an original and meaningful relationship to the world, a personal viewpoint that would salvage his deeply religious sensibility and lend aid to his pressing emotional needs. Since Christianity could no longer serve these needs, he attempted to find a new synthesis through Germanic idealism, Hindu theosophy, Confucian ethics, poetic romanticism, and his inescapable background of rugged Yankee individualism. His belief in the primacy of personality, his admiration (like Carlyle's) of heroes, his definitely human-centered, anthropocentric, aristocratic orientation is repeated over and over, throughout his many basic essays. "No object really interests us," he wrote, "but man, and in man only his superiorities; and though we are aware of a perfect law in nature, it has fascination for us only through its relation to him, or as it is rooted in the mind." (*Representative Men*)

Like the German idealists, Emerson could not abide the dichotomies of life—those troublesome divisions between reality and illusion, mind and nature, religion and science, moral law and physical law, the temporal and the eternal, the spiritual ideal and the mundane actual. His version of philosophic idealism, which he called Transcendentalism—borrowing the term from Kant—was an effort to override or *transcend* these dualisms through the identification of Mind (always capitalized) with Spirit (likewise), and the equation of both with Absolute Spirit which in turn becomes another term for—the World, the Universe, the All-in-One. That equation is *correspondence*: the human soul, said Emerson, corresponds to (is potentially identical with) everything that exists. Everything. (And what else is there?) Like Hegel and the Hindu mystics, Emerson saw the apparent division between the one and the many, the self and the other, as only a form of mischief created by *Maya*, the power of illusion. If we can transcend the illusory belief in difference and material objects then man and nature will be reunited, reintegrated, recoalesced, and History (capitalized) or God, or the Over-Soul, aided by the achievements of human culture, particularly romantic poetry and idealistic philosophy, will again be merged with the human mind, with the world of material tangible things, with all that is.

But what then about evil in this merging of mind and nature, this correspondence of human and the Over-Soul? Like the Christian theologians, Emerson and his fellow Transcendentalists were still bedeviled by that nagging old question. How explain slavery, the suffering of children, the atrocities of war, in a panspiritualistic universe based on Pre-established Harmony? It's not easy; and Emerson resorts like others of his essentially tender-minded character to the equally ancient doctrine of appearance, illusion, temporality. Evil, he says, is only apparent evil—in reality what appears to us as evil is meant for the greater good of the whole; in the long run each seemingly evil event is counterbalanced by the universal good, the ultimate self-harmony of mind: your mind, my mind, God's mind, all three being parts of the same greater Whole anyhow. Never mind the screams of the suffering: it's only *Maya*. This tortured and tortuous metaphysical hallucination forms the basis of Emerson's lifelong optimism—what he calls the "law of compensation." But whereas the professional philosophers of both East and West, India and Europe, tried to persuade us toward this doctrine through systematic and rational exposition, thus tying themselves into hopeless and helpless knots of Gordian complexity, Emerson avoided the rational approach by putting the whole intricate intellectual contraption into poetry and into the poetical prose of his essays—exactly where it belongs. Emerson appeals not to experience, logic, sense or common sense, but to our innate idealism, our instinctive need for harmony and meaningfulness, a need which grows greater when the world grows more desperate. Emerson offers us not tuition, as he liked to say, but the power of intuition—which has this great charm, that through intuition we can discover whatever it is we most *want* to discover.

Emerson the Poet-Essayist

My summary of Emerson's ideas may tend to make them look faintly ridiculous, as it seems to me they are. But the man himself was not ridiculous, and in his essays, obscure and rhapsodical though they be, certain lines leap out at us and ring in the mind.

From *Nature*:

The foregoing generations beheld God and nature face to face; we, through their eyes. Why should not we also enjoy an original relation to the universe?

Nature is the symbol of spirit.

Who looks upon a river and is not reminded of the flux of all things?

The corruption of man is followed by the corruption of language.

The mind is a part of the nature of things; the world is a divine dream.

A man is a god in ruins.

To the wise . . . a fact is true poetry.

Build . . . your own world.

From *The American Scholar*:

The scholar is the delegated intellect. In the right state he is Man Thinking.

The scholar of the first age received into him the world around. . . . It came into him life; it went out from him truth.

Genius looks forward; the eyes of man are set in his forehead . . .

Action is with the scholar subordinate but it is also essential. Without it he is not yet a man.

There is creative reading as well as creative writing.

Character is higher than intellect.

The scholar is the world's eye. He is the world's heart.

The world is his who can see through its pretension.

Not he is great who can alter matter but he who can alter my state of mind.

The world is nothing, the man is all; in yourself is the law of all nature.

From *Self-Reliance*:

In every work of genius we recognize our own rejected thoughts. They come back to us with a certain alienated majesty.

Trust thyself: every heart vibrates to that iron string.

Whoso would be a man must be a nonconformist. . . .
Nothing is at last sacred but the integrity of your own mind.

Truth is handsomer than the affectation of love.

It is easy in the world to live after the world's opinion; it
is easy in solitude to live after our own; but the great man
is he who in the midst of the crowd keeps with perfect sweet-
ness the independence of solitude.

A foolish consistency is the hobgoblin of little minds. . . .
With consistency a great soul has simply nothing to do. He
may as well concern himself with his shadow on the
wall. . . . To be great is to be misunderstood.

An institution is the lengthened shadow of one man.

We must go alone. I like the silent church before the
service begins better than any preaching.

Prayer is the contemplation of the facts of life from the
highest point of view.

All men plume themselves on the improvement of society,
and no man improves.

Nothing can bring you peace but yourself. Nothing can
bring you peace but the triumph of principles.

From *Society and Solitude*:

If you would learn to write, 'tis in the street you must learn
it. . . . The people, and not the college, is the writer's home.

From *Experience*:

The true romance which the world exists to realize will be the transformation of genius into practical power.

From *The Over-Soul*:

The faith that stands on authority is not faith. The reliance on authority measures the decline of religion, the withdrawal of the soul.

Humanity shines in Homer, in Chaucer, in Spenser, in Shakespeare, in Milton. They are content with truth. They use the positive degree. They seem frigid and phlegmatic to those who have been spiced with the frantic passion and violent coloring of inferior but popular writers.

Man is a stream whose source is hidden.

We see the world piece by piece, as the sun, the moon, the tree, the animal; but the whole, of which these are the shining parts, is the soul.

Our faith comes in moments; our vice is habitual.

We live in succession, in division, in parts, in particles. Meantime within man is the soul of the whole, the wise silence, the universal beauty . . . the eternal ONE.

And so forth. Emerson was the first great American writer, "the father of us all," as Susan Sontag (of all people!) has said. Without Emerson there would have been only a lesser Thoreau and maybe no Walt Whitman at all. The concerns of Emerson are the concerns of most writers today, particularly American writers. The search for transcendence and integrity and truth goes on, as witness the work of Annie Dillard, Wendell Berry, Cormac McCarthy, Larry McMurtry, Leslie Silko, Peter Matthiessen, Barry Lopez, Edward Hoagland, and Jim Harrison, among many others.

Nor was Emerson merely a closet radical, a secluded dreamer, a temporizing bystander in human affairs. When the occasion demanded, he could rise to action—at least to the action of public speech and open protest, which is really about all that we can expect from poets and philosophers. Emerson opposed slavery and supported the abolitionists, including John Brown, at a time when it was dangerous to do so. Emerson spoke out in opposition to the war of conquest against Mexico and did what he could to prevent the forcible removal of the Cherokee Indians from their ancestral homeland in North Carolina. He attacked the great "statesman" Daniel Webster when that pompous, petulant, compromising windbag, ballooning at the height of his fame, was defending the Fugitive Slave Law in Congress. Emerson was a man of intellectual courage, never afraid to speak his mind; this is a quality not too common among professional scribes. Emerson may have been a bore as well—but he was a brave and honest bore. And he was ours.

Nature Love

Sportsmen

How to Use Your
SIRENIA Wildlife Caller

*T*he SIRENIA is not meant to sound like a bobcat, coyote, or fox. It is tuned so the caller can reproduce the cries of a trapped or injured cottontail or jackrabbit.

Hold the end of the caller in the V formed by the thumb and the palm of your hand so that you can muffle or amplify the sound by closing and opening your hand.

Always blow from the diaphragm rather than puffing out your cheeks. This method gives you much better breath control which, of course, makes your calling more realistic and produces better results.

Close hand over end of caller and blow hard, opening the hand at the same time. Make the first few screams loud and terrified, then let the screams trail off, as if from exhaustion, ending with whimpering cries that gradually fade out. Wait about a minute and then repeat the entire series.

When you spot an animal approaching while you're calling, it is best to stop calling and let him come into closer range. If he should stop too far out, or begin circling, use either the whimpering tone or give a few squeaks with the SIRENIA close-range COAXER. Even an animal that is running away usually can be stopped and turned for a standing shot by this technique.

If you call an animal and make a kill, don't expose yourself or make any movements or noise. Predators frequently run in pairs or even families, and it is not unusual to call two or more from the same stand. This is especially true with coyote and with fox in late summer and early fall, less likely with bobcat.

The range of the SIRENIA will amaze you. Predators can hear it a mile or more away, depending upon the terrain.

The SIRENIA close-range COAXER is best used with short, fast squeaks sounding like a mouse. This is very effective when the predator is close and you wish to maneuver him into a more favorable position or bring him in even closer. It can be held between the fingers of the hand on the forearm of the rifle or shotgun. . . .

Night Calling

Predatory animals are more easily called in at night, because they normally do most of their hunting at night. (However, it is more sporting and a better test of your skill as a hunter to call them during the day.) It is best when calling at night for two hunters to stand back to back in a small clearing, each with a good light held with the brightest part of the beam a few feet above ground level and move the beam slowly back and forth. You will be able to see the eyes shine in the fringe of the beam. Don't put the bright part of the beam on the animal until you are ready to shoot. When you put the bright light in the animal's eyes he will usually stop for a moment and give you a standing shot. . . .

Calling Bobcat

When calling in bobcat country you must be especially watchful as bobcats usually come in more cautiously than any other predators and will take full advantage of all available cover in approaching the caller. . . . Bobcats are very curious and are apt to stand and watch the caller for several minutes (provided there is no quick movement or sudden noise), thus giving you a standing shot. Bobcats are more wary than other predators and if you call one and kill it or miss there is very little chance of calling another or calling back the one you missed from the same stand. . . . Practice will increase your percentage of cats called and killed.

Calling Coyotes

Coyotes probably provide more thrills and excitement for the caller than any other predator as they usually come in very fast and it is not unusual to call them within ten feet or less. . . . If the coyote is on a wrong course or you want to stop him in a favorable spot, give a low, piteous cry on your caller or a couple of squeezes on your SIRENIA close-range COAXER. Coyotes often run in pairs or even families, so if you call one and make a kill, keep calling. . . .

Calling Fox

Foxes are probably the greatest suckers of all for a predator call. Once you convince a fox that there is a rabbit in distress, you almost have to kick him in the teeth to unconvince him.

In fox country it isn't unusual to call and kill several, one after another. If you call a fox and miss or only wound him, keep calling because it's sometimes possible to call him back.

Calling Mountain Lions

Without question, the mountain lion is the most difficult of all North American game to hunt without dogs. They are the top trophy for the wild-animal caller. They are fewer in number than any other predator and the caller should know the animal, its habits and the country. Mountain lions are great travelers, except the female when she has small cubs.

Hints to Help You Call

When using your car to travel from one stand to another, try to park it quietly and in a low spot or other concealment. Don't slam car doors.

Always walk into the wind away from your car for at least a hundred yards before taking a stand.

If there is a tree handy in which you can sit comfortably, and just high enough for good visibility, it will be an advantage as predators don't usually look up into trees.

Blend into the natural cover of the country in which you are hunting. Use a blind or camouflage clothing, grease paint (green or brown) on face and hands, and scents to kill the human odor.

When an animal is sighted coming in, don't be in a hurry to shoot; let him come closer for a better shot. Sometimes there may be two, in which case you may get a double. Shoot the one farthest away first and the closer one before he gets out of range.

Don't give up easily; predator calling will have good as well as bad days, just like any other type of hunting.

Let us know about your calling experiences. If you have any questions, we will do our best to answer them for you.

Good luck and good calling.

It's Results That Count!

Jim Slothrop and Doug Riddell used SIRENIA callers to win the 1961 Arizona Field contest by calling up and killing 264 coyotes, 8 bobcats, and 5 fox. During 18 weekends of calling they called up and killed 495 coyotes, 10 bobcats, and 6 fox. This record has never been excelled.

SIRENIA has won more major field contests throughout the West than any other varmint caller. These wins are too numerous to mention.

[Author's Note: The above are verbatim excerpts from an anonymous printed leaflet found on a dirt road in central Arizona. All of the target animals mentioned here, except the coyote, are rare or endangered species. All but the mountain lion prey chiefly on rodents, snakes, hares, and rabbits. The mountain lion is a deer hunter. Also found, and collected, in the vicinity of the dropped leaflet, were three Pepsi-Cola cans, two 7-Up cans, one empty whiskey bottle (Old Crow), about a dozen discharged twenty-gauge shotgun shells, many wads of pink Kleenex, one Pampers plastic throwaway diaper (loaded), a plastic spoon, and one blue dacron sock, worn, size ten.]